HOW TO DRAW
MANGA CHIBIS
& CUTE CRITTERS

Written & Illustrated by Samantha Whitten & Jeannie Lee

Q Quarto Knows

Brimming with creative inspiration, how-to projects, and useful information to enrich your everyday life, Quarto Knows is a favorite destination for those pursuing their interests and passions. Visit our site and dig deeper with our books into your area of interest: Quarto Creates, Quarto Cooks, Quarto Homes, Quarto Lives, Quarto Drives, Quarto Explores, Quarto Gifts, or Quarto Kids.

Inspiring | Educating | Creating | Entertaining

First Published in 2011 by Walter Foster Publishing, an imprint of The Quarto Group.
6 Orchard Road, Suite 100, Lake Forest, CA 92630, USA.
T (949) 380-7510 F (949) 380-7575 www.QuartoKnows.com

Walter Foster Publishing titles are also available at discount for retail, wholesale, promotional, and bulk purchase. For details, contact the Special Sales Manager by email at specialsales@quarto.com or by mail at The Quarto Group, Attn: Special Sales Manager, 401 Second Avenue North, Suite 310, Minneapolis, MN 55401, USA.

ISBN: 978-1-60058-290-5

Printed in China
11

TABLE OF CONTENTS

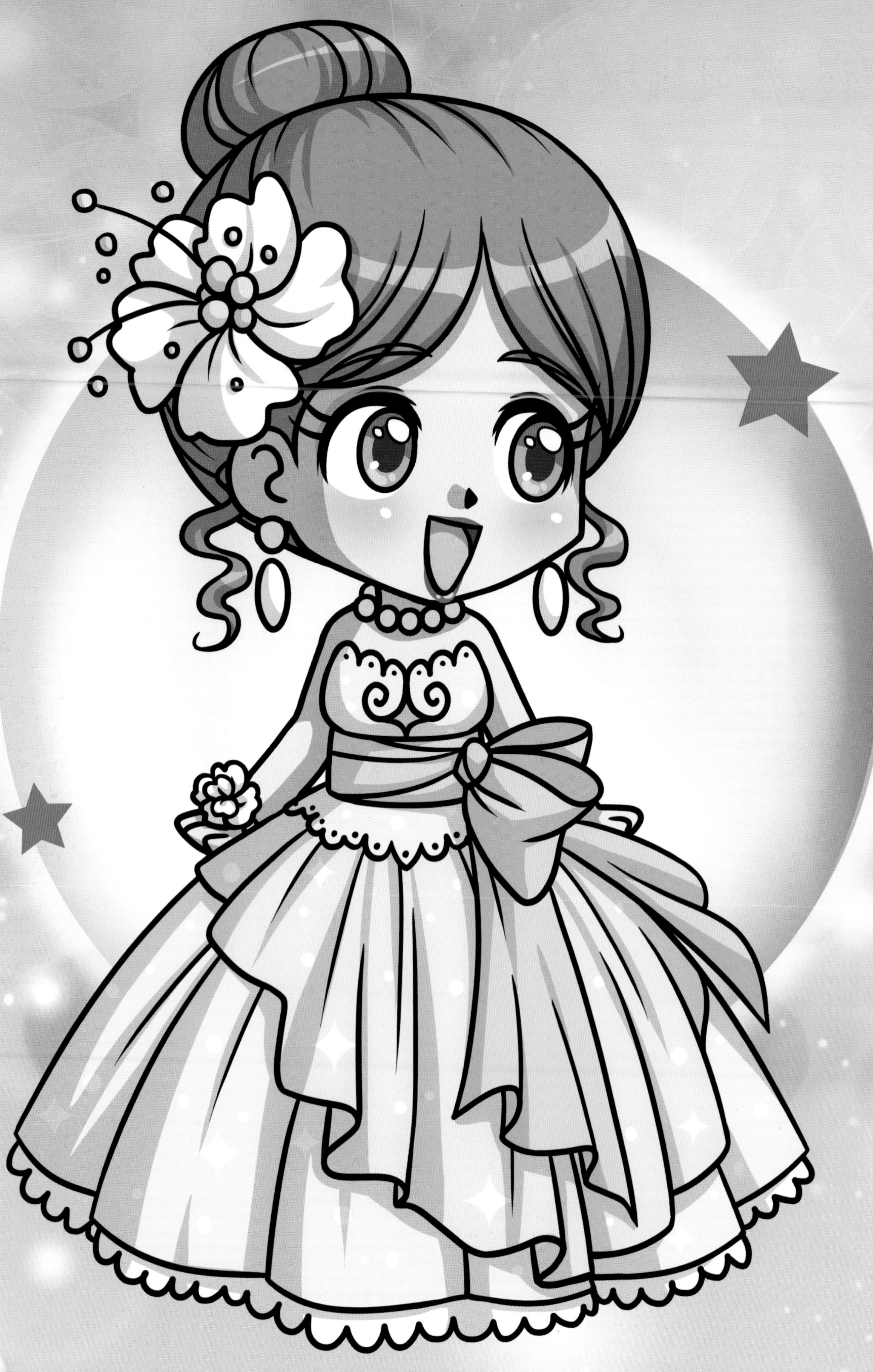

INTRODUCTION

You know them well—you're reading your favorite manga or watching an anime, and suddenly a chibi appears. The word *chibis* (pronounced "chee-bees") means "little" in Japanese. Chibis are super cute caricatures of people or animals that have been shrunken and squashed into funny, childlike creatures with big heads, stubby proportions, and silly expressions. In this book, you'll learn to draw all sorts of chibis. You'll also discover exactly what gives them their "chibiness," including proportions, facial features, expressions, and poses, as well as how to "chibify" props, furniture, and other background elements. And because companion critters are a common theme in anime and manga, you'll also learn to transform common animal friends into chibis. If that weren't enough, this book even comes with your very own guides, who will accompany you on your artistic journey to cuteness along the way. Meet Sakura, Takashi, and Poko-chan below.

Nobody works harder than Takashi. He takes his schoolwork very seriously and can be a bit grumpy sometimes.

Poko-chan is a magical little creature whose favorite hobby is eating. Watch out or he'll eat your lunch!

Sakura is a hyper, fun-loving cat girl who craves adventure and tries to be friends with everybody.

So what are you waiting for? A world of adorable chibis awaits! In the name of cuteness, let's dive in and get started!

TOOLS & MATERIALS

The artwork in this book was drawn and colored on a computer, but don't worry if you're not set up for that. You can create all of the projects featured in this book with traditional media, such as pencils, colored pencils, pens, crayons, and paints. Below are the supplies you may want to have handy to get started.

SKETCHPAD & DRAWING PAPER Sketchpads and inexpensive printer paper are great for working out your ideas.

TRACING PAPER Tracing paper is useful for tracing figures and creating a clean version of a sketch using a light box. (See "How to Use a Light Box," page 7.) Use quality tracing paper that is sturdy enough to handle erasing and coloring.

CARDSTOCK Cardstock is sturdier than thinner printer paper, which makes it ideal for drawing on repeatedly or for heavy-duty artwork.

▼ BLACK FINE LINE MARKER Use a black fine line marker to tighten your lines and add the finishing touch to your final color artwork.

▲ PENCILS Pencil lead, or graphite, varies in darkness and hardness. Pencils with a number and an H have harder graphite, which marks paper more lightly. Pencils with a number and a B mean the graphite is softer and looks darker on paper. We recommend H or HB pencils (HB pencils are equivalent to No. 2 pencils) for sketching exercises. In general, use harder pencils (H) for lighter, thinner lines. Use softer pencils (B) for bolder, thicker lines.

▼ ERASERS A vinyl eraser and a kneaded eraser are both good to have on hand. A vinyl eraser is white and rubbery; it's softer and gentler on paper than a pink eraser. A kneaded eraser is like putty in that you can mold it into shapes to erase small areas. You can also gently "blot" a sketch with a kneaded eraser to lighten the artwork.

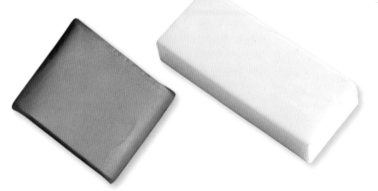

▶ **ART MARKERS** Art markers are perfect for adding bold, vibrant color to your artwork. They are great for shading and laying down large areas of color.

▲ **PENS** Different inks work well for coloring. When buying pens, look for "waterproof" or "archival ink" printed on the side of the pen. Look for pens that release ink consistently for inking line art over sketches.

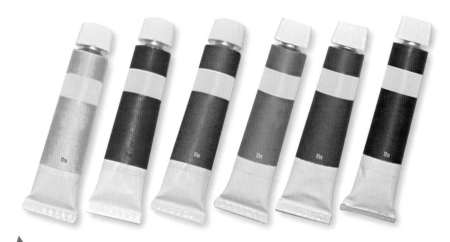

▲ **COLORED PENCILS** Colored pencils layer over each other easily. They are user friendly, and some are even erasable!

◀ **PAINTS** Have fun exploring acrylic, water-color, or good old-fashioned poster paint. Make sure to research what types of paper work well with each paint.

HOW TO USE A LIGHT BOX

A light box is a useful and generally inexpensive tool (although there are fancier, professional-grade versions). As its name suggests, a light box is a compact box with a transparent top and light inside. The light illuminates papers placed on top, allowing dark lines to show through for easy tracing. Simply tape your rough drawing on the surface of the light box. Place a clean sheet of paper over your original sketch and turn the box on. The light illuminates the drawing underneath and will help you accurately trace the lines onto the new sheet of paper. You can also create a similar effect by placing a lamp under a glass table or taping your sketch and drawing paper to a clear glass window and using natural light.

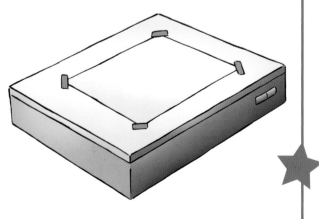

DRAWING TECHNIQUES

WARMING UP

Warm up your hand by drawing random lines, scribbles, and squiggles. Familiarize yourself with the different lines that your pencils can create, and experiment with every stroke you can think of, using both a sharp point and a dull point.

TYPES OF STROKES

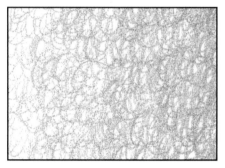

CIRCULAR Move your pencil in a circular motion, either randomly (shown here) or in patterned rows. For denser coverage, overlap the circles. Varying the pressure creates different textures.

LINEAR Move your pencil in the same direction, whether vertically, horizontally, or diagonally. Strokes can be short and choppy or long and even.

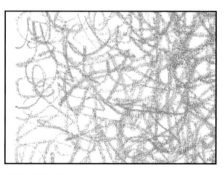

SCUMBLING Scribble your pencil in random strokes to create an organic mass. Changing the pressure and the amount of time you linger over the same area can increase or decrease the value of the color.

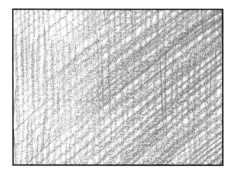

HATCHING Sketch a series of roughly parallel lines. The closer the lines are to each other, the denser and darker the color. Crosshatching involves laying one set of hatched lines over another, but in a different direction.

SMOOTH No matter what stroke you use, if you control the pencil, you can produce an even layer of color. You can also blend your strokes so that you can't tell how color was applied.

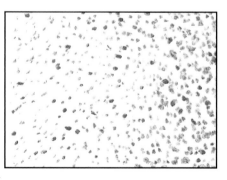

STIPPLING Sharpen your pencil and apply small dots all over the area. For denser coverage, apply the dots closer together.

COLOR BASICS

Color can help bring your drawings to life, but first it helps to know a bit about color theory. There are three *primary* colors: red, yellow, and blue. These colors cannot be created by mixing other colors. Mixing two primary colors produces a *secondary* color: orange, green, and purple. Mixing a primary color with a secondary color produces a *tertiary* color: red-orange, red-purple, yellow-orange, yellow-green, blue-green, and blue-purple. Reds, yellows, and oranges are "warm" colors; greens, blues, and purples are "cool" colors. See the color combinations below for more mixing ideas.

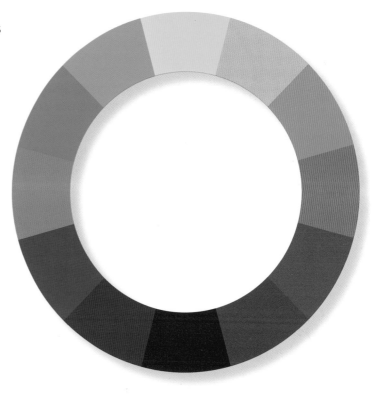

THE COLOR WHEEL

A color wheel is useful for understanding relationships between colors. Knowing where each color is located on the color wheel makes it easy to understand how colors relate to and react with one another.

EASY COLOR COMBINATIONS

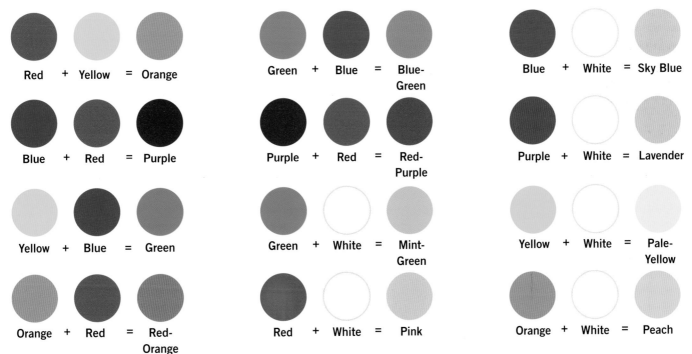

Red + Yellow = Orange

Blue + Red = Purple

Yellow + Blue = Green

Orange + Red = Red-Orange

Green + Blue = Blue-Green

Purple + Red = Red-Purple

Green + White = Mint-Green

Red + White = Pink

Blue + White = Sky Blue

Purple + White = Lavender

Yellow + White = Pale-Yellow

Orange + White = Peach

ADDING COLOR TO YOUR DRAWING

Some artists draw directly on illustration board or watercolor paper and then apply color directly to the original pencil drawing; however, if you are a beginning artist, you might opt to preserve your original pencil drawing by making several photocopies and applying color to a photocopy. This way, you'll always have your original drawing in case you make a mistake or you want to experiment with different colors or mediums.

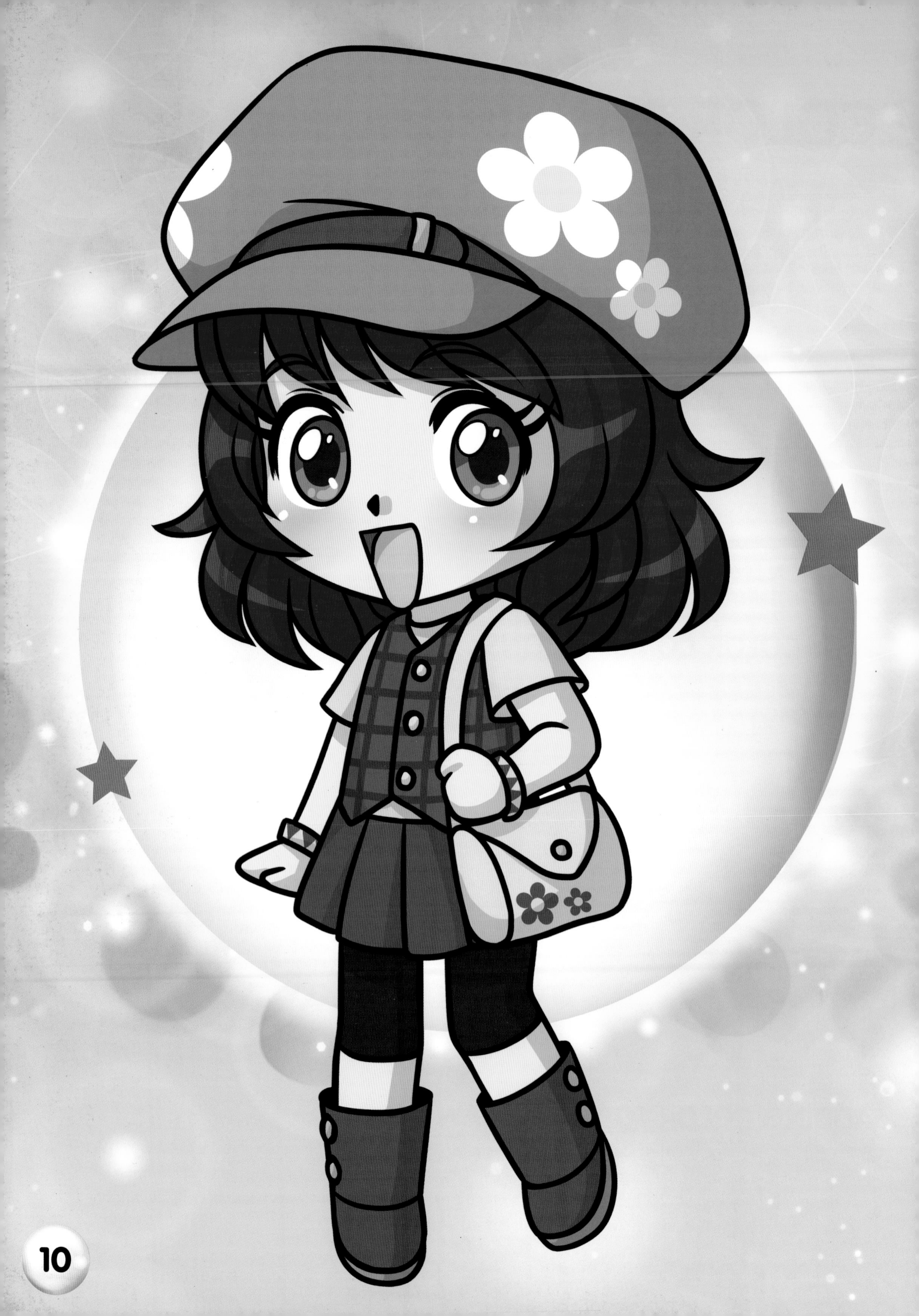

CHAPTER 1
CHIBI BASICS

WHAT MAKES IT A CHIBI?

The one attribute that sets chibis apart from other anime or manga characters is their proportions. They are squashed and simplified, and their features and sizes are altered to make them look as cute as possible. Common traits include an oversized head, a small body, stubby limbs, and big eyes.

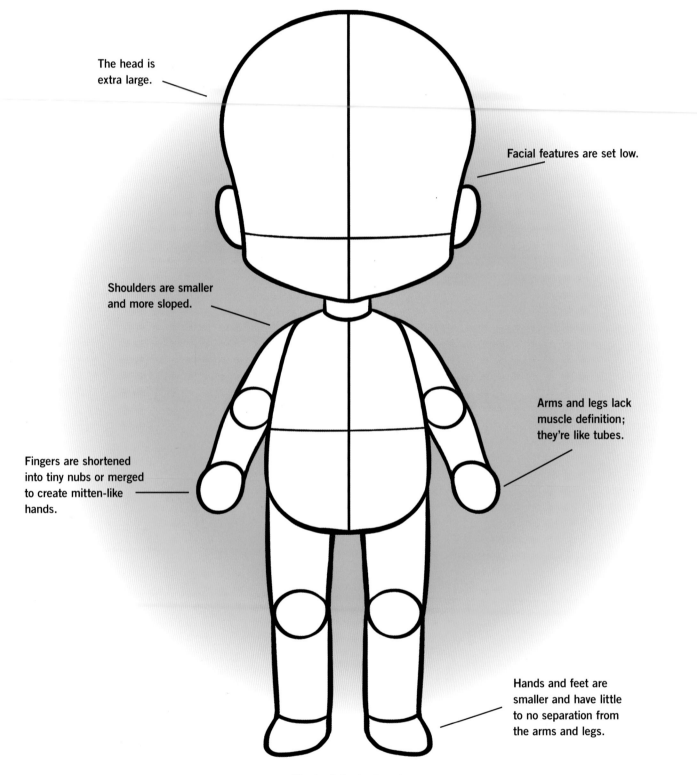

The head is extra large.

Facial features are set low.

Shoulders are smaller and more sloped.

Arms and legs lack muscle definition; they're like tubes.

Fingers are shortened into tiny nubs or merged to create mitten-like hands.

Hands and feet are smaller and have little to no separation from the arms and legs.

The body is shortened.

BASIC CONSTRUCTION

These diagrams illustrate how the proportions of a normal-sized character are different from those of a chibi. A chibi's head is several times larger than a normal head, with lower guidelines for the facial features. Additionally, a chibi's arms and legs are half the typical length. In fact, a chibi's arms are so short that the chibi can't reach the top of its own head! Body parts are chubbier and rounder in chibi form, but this doesn't necessarily mean the character is fatter. Chibis can be chubby, skinny, muscular—any body type. Next to a normal figure, a chibi may resemble a child, even if it's not. A chibi character is merely a simplified version of a normal-sized character.

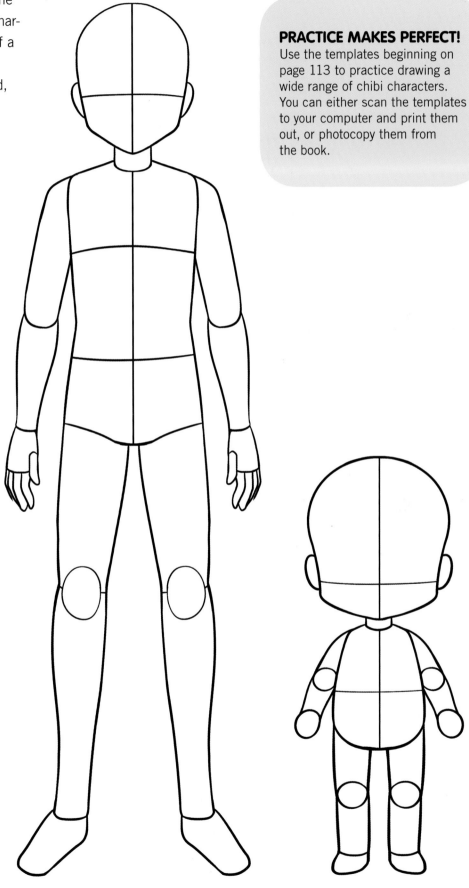

PRACTICE MAKES PERFECT!
Use the templates beginning on page 113 to practice drawing a wide range of chibi characters. You can either scan the templates to your computer and print them out, or photocopy them from the book.

CHIBI GIRL TRAITS

Because chibis lack physical definition by nature, poses and character traits typically indicate their gender. Girl chibis, for example, have cute, feminine poses. They're commonly drawn hopping, skipping, or floating in midair to demonstrate that they're light on their feet. The "pigeon-toe" pose is common for female chibi characters. Toes pointing inward give the character a coy demeanor. In contrast to a male chibi body, females may also have hourglass figures.

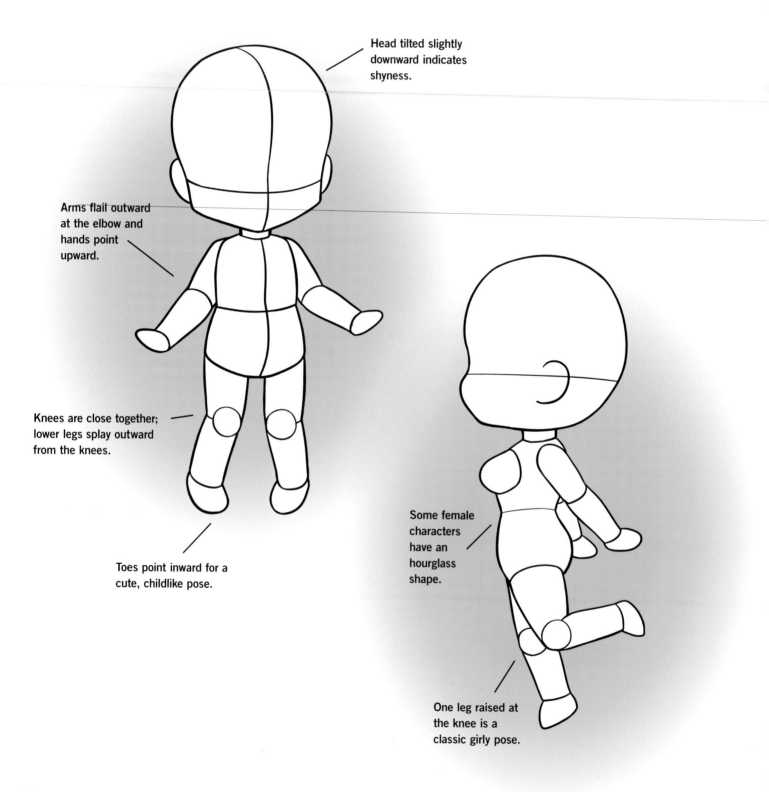

Head tilted slightly downward indicates shyness.

Arms flail outward at the elbow and hands point upward.

Knees are close together; lower legs splay outward from the knees.

Toes point inward for a cute, childlike pose.

Some female characters have an hourglass shape.

One leg raised at the knee is a classic girly pose.

CHIBI BOY TRAITS

Chibi boys typically have stronger, firmer poses. A male chibi character often stands with his chest puffed out, legs slightly apart, and feet planted firmly on the ground. Arms are often drawn in strong or casual poses, with the hands on the hips or the arms hanging straight down. Hands can be drawn as fists, which are merely ball shapes. The male chibi body shape is generally more rectangular than the female chibi body shape. For a more muscular character, however, you can make the chest wider and the hips narrower. Muscles are often smoothed down, as definition is contrary to the chibi style—unless your character happens to be a super body builder!

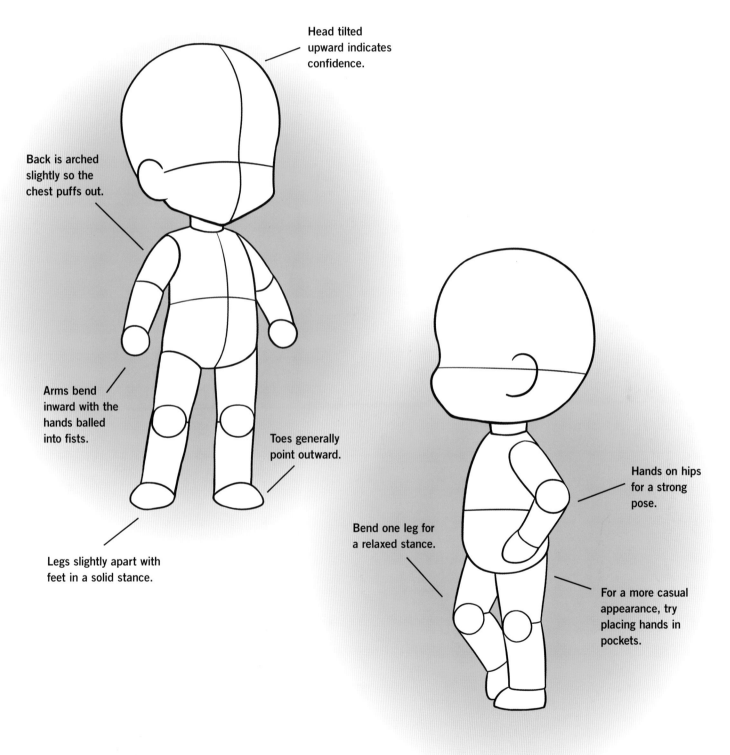

Head tilted upward indicates confidence.

Back is arched slightly so the chest puffs out.

Arms bend inward with the hands balled into fists.

Toes generally point outward.

Legs slightly apart with feet in a solid stance.

Hands on hips for a strong pose.

Bend one leg for a relaxed stance.

For a more casual appearance, try placing hands in pockets.

BREAKING IT DOWN: SAKURA

To see the differences between a normal figure and chibi figure more clearly, let's take a look at them side by side. The differences between the two figures are many, but they still look like the same character because they share traits unique to Sakura, including hairstyle, colors, outfit, and body language. It's important to figure out which traits to keep the same and which to exaggerate so your character looks like the same person whether it's in normal or chibi form.

HEAD

The chibi head is much wider than the head on the normal figure; moreover, the facial features are placed much lower on the head. A chibi barely has a chin, and the eyes are larger and set wider apart. The eyes are also positioned lower on the head, which means the nose, which is smaller, is between the eyes instead of below them. Some artists omit the nose altogether.

BODY

The chibi body transforms from a rectangle to a pear shape (wider on the bottom and narrow at the shoulders). The arms show no definition at the elbows, and the hands are wedges with lines to indicate stubby fingers. The chibi chest is much smaller, and there are fewer folds in the clothing. Notice how the pleated skirt becomes little more than wedges of color. The tail is shorter and only has a single curl.

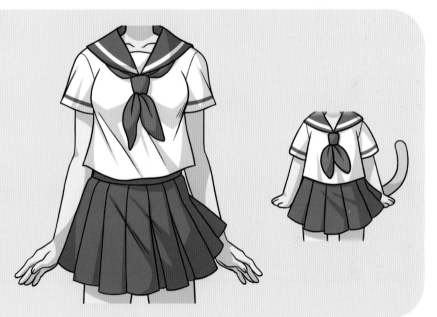

LEGS

Goodbye legs, hello noodles! Avoid adding too much detail to chibi legs. In chibi form, the thigh muscles and lower legs disappear completely—only shading indicates the knees. Think of chibi legs as long tubes with bends in the middle. The shoes are smaller and stubbier, as well. Chibi Sakura adopts a pigeon-toe stance, with her knees close together and legs angled outward.

BREAKING IT DOWN: TAKASHI

Now that we've changed Sakura into a chibi, let's move on to her grumpy friend, Takashi. The breakdown for males is pretty much the same as it is for females, although there are slight differences.

HEAD

Takashi's chibi head is wider and larger overall. The eyes are oversized, set wider apart, and placed lower on the head, while his ears are rounder with simplified details. The nose is a small dot. Flushed cheeks is a universal chibi trait.

BODY

Takashi's body is wider at the bottom and narrow at the top, with slim, sloping shoulders. In chibi form, he appears to be a little chubby in the belly, which gives the look of having "baby fat"—another childlike feature common in chibi styles. The folds of his clothing have also been refined, and his hands are also balled into little fists.

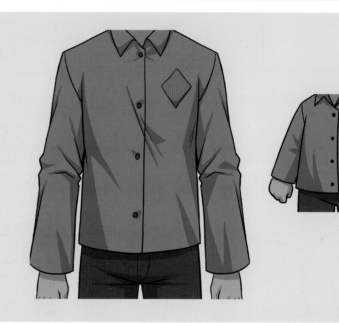

LEGS

The knees have vanished again! Takashi's chibi legs are straight and simplified. Similarly, clothing folds are smooth. Takashi's chibi feet are the same shape as Sakura's, but the pose is more masculine.

BASIC CHIBI FACE

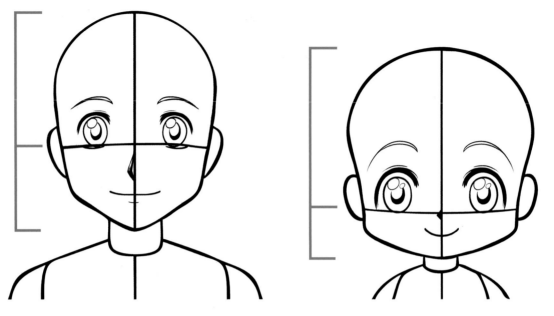

FRONT VIEW

Compared to a normal face, chibi facial features are larger and sit toward the bottom half of the face. The forehead is large, and the eyes are wider and set below the center of the face. Chibi eyebrows arch more dramatically around the shape of the eyes, resulting in a wide-eyed, childlike expression. The chibi nose is a tiny triangle, and the mouth is shorter. Also note the rounder, wider head; flattened chin; and short, thin neck. Use the blue guidelines to measure the differences in proportion and placement between the upper and lower halves of each face.

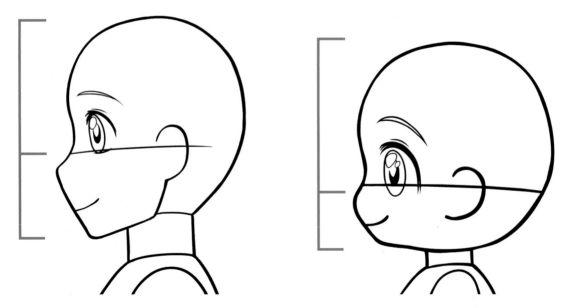

SIDE VIEW

In the side view, also called the profile view, the facial features are still compact and placed lower on the face, resulting in a larger, broader forehead. The jawline and chin are smoothed out and simplified, which makes the chibi character appear shorter and pudgier. The head is more circular, whereas the eye and eyebrow are larger and more pronounced. A small protruding bump indicates the nose, and the mouth and neck are both shorter. You'll also notice the ear doesn't connect to the edge of the jawline.

AVERAGE CHIBI BODY

Chibis come in all shapes, sizes, and proportions, but the most common body shape is shown at right. In this example, the body and legs are approximately the same height, and the head is larger than both! Artists often invent their own measurements and proportions, and we encourage you to do the same. If your chibis do start to resemble normal-sized children, tweak the image. Making the head larger is a good first step.

The four most common angles are the front, side (profile), back, and three-quarter views. Note how the shapes of the face change from each angle, and how the arms and legs indicate which direction the character is facing. Even if the angles change, the character still appears to be the same shape, height, and size from all views.

TIP

Use basic shapes, including circles, cylinders, and guidelines, to start your drawings. Skipping this step may result in your characters appearing out of proportion.

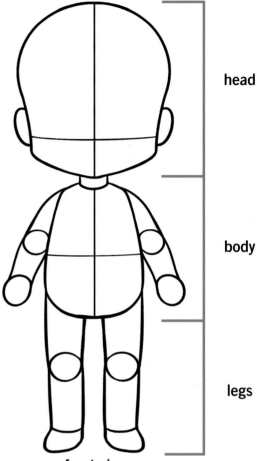

head

body

legs

front view

side view

back view

3/4 view

CHIBI GIRL FACE

The preliminary steps for drawing boy and girl chibis are essentially the same. As you become more experienced, explore ways to enhance each character's gender.

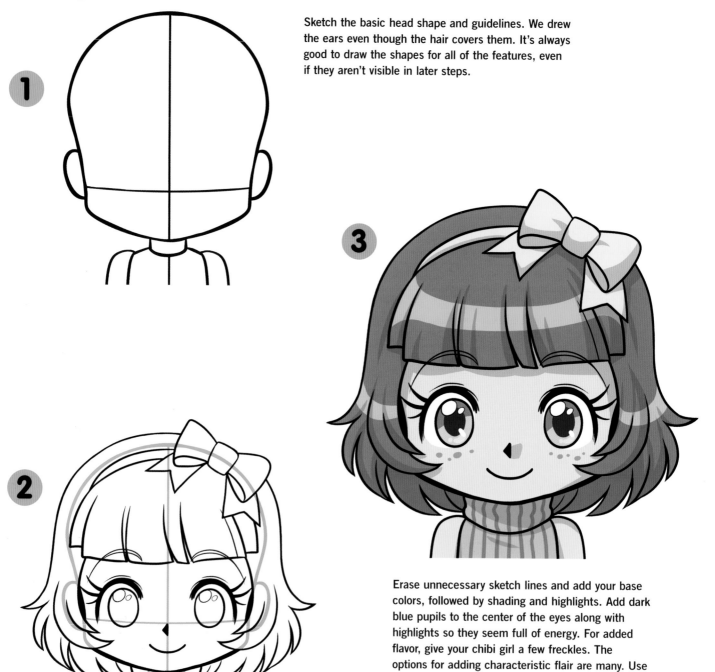

1 Sketch the basic head shape and guidelines. We drew the ears even though the hair covers them. It's always good to draw the shapes for all of the features, even if they aren't visible in later steps.

2 Draw the eyes, eyebrows, and eyelashes. Next draw the hair, mouth, nose, and accessories. Pay attention to how the guidelines help establish where the other details sit.

3 Erase unnecessary sketch lines and add your base colors, followed by shading and highlights. Add dark blue pupils to the center of the eyes along with highlights so they seem full of energy. For added flavor, give your chibi girl a few freckles. The options for adding characteristic flair are many. Use your imagination!

CHIBI BOY FACE

1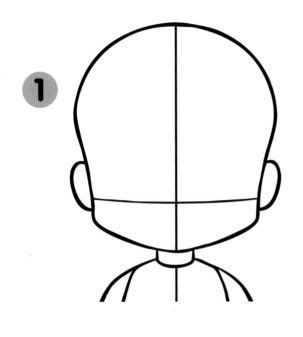

Sketch the basic head shape and guidelines. Make sure the boy's shoulders are broader than the girl's.

3

Erase unnecessary guidelines. Then add your colors and highlights. You can give the boy brown hair and green eyes, or any colors you like. Add highlights to his hair to make it appear shiny and round. With dark green pupils and brighter highlights, his eyes seem alert. Add a pink flush to his cheeks so he appears as if he's been playing outside.

2

Add the eyes, noticing how the boy's eyes rest directly on the centerline, whereas the girl's eyes are set slightly lower. The boy doesn't have eyelashes, but he does have thicker eyebrows. Next, add the nose and mouth, remembering to leave more space on the chin area than you would on a girl chibi. Add a boyish hairstyle, with two little tufts standing on end.

CHIBI GIRL FACE: SIDE VIEW

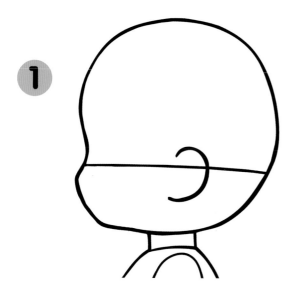

① Begin with basic shapes and guidelines, including a rounded head and slight bump for the nose. This is fairly typical for both boy and girl chibis. The chin is short and slightly angles outward. Because this is a profile view, the ear sits near the center of the head.

② Draw the eye first, placing it toward the lower half of the face. Next, add in the details, including the mouth, hair, and accessories. Don't get discouraged if it takes some practice to capture the style.

③ Erase the guidelines and clean up your line art.

④ Match the colors and highlights to the front view chibi, or add all new colors if you like.

24

CHIBI BOY FACE: SIDE VIEW

1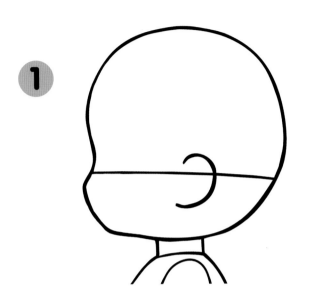

Begin as before with basic shapes and guidelines. As with the front view, add slightly more space on the lower half of the boy's face.

2

Reference the front view of the boy's facial features, hair, and clothes as you draw him at a different angle. Pay attention to where the top of the hair is in relation to the guideline.

3

Next, erase the basic shapes and guidelines, and clean up your line art.

4

Reference the front view drawing as you color, shade, and highlight. Add a smooth highlight arc on the head to create depth. Don't forget to add a slight flush to his cheek as a finishing touch.

CHIBI BODY: FRONT VIEW

The front view is ideal when first designing a character, because you can see the entire body. To draw a more lively front view than a standing chibi offers, try moving body parts or changing stances. Raise the character's arms, bend its legs, or give it a quirky expression. There are many ways to add feeling to a seemingly straightforward pose. In this example, our chibi girl has been caught by surprise!

First, draw the basic shapes: cylinders, circles, and guidelines.

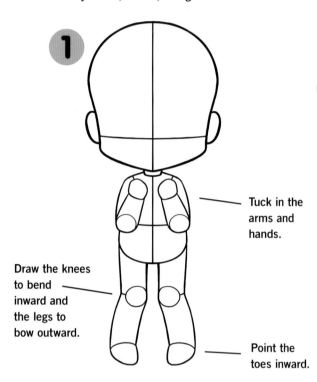

1

Tuck in the arms and hands.

Draw the knees to bend inward and the legs to bow outward.

Point the toes inward.

2

Draw the facial features, hair, clothes, and accessories.

3

Add solid colors before shading or highlighting. Color in the pupils and add highlights to give the eyes depth. Add a blush to her cheeks, if you like.

CHIBI BODY: SIDE VIEW

Use guidelines to keep the side view chibi from appearing flat. There are tricks to add dimension. For example, draw the arm and leg on the opposite side so they are visible. Always think three-dimensionally!

1 Draw the basic shapes and guidelines. Remember: Heads are round!

Notice that you can see the right arm and right leg even from the left side.

2 Draw the facial features, hair, clothes, and fingers so they appear to wrap around the guidelines.

3 Add color, shading, and highlights.

EXERCISE YOUR CREATIVITY!
Remember that fantasy characters can have features that are unnatural in the real world. Why *not* make their hair blue and their eyes yellow? These unexpected surprises make your character unique and fun.

CHIBI BODY: BACK VIEW

The back view is essentially the same as the front view. The basic shapes are the same—only the details are different.

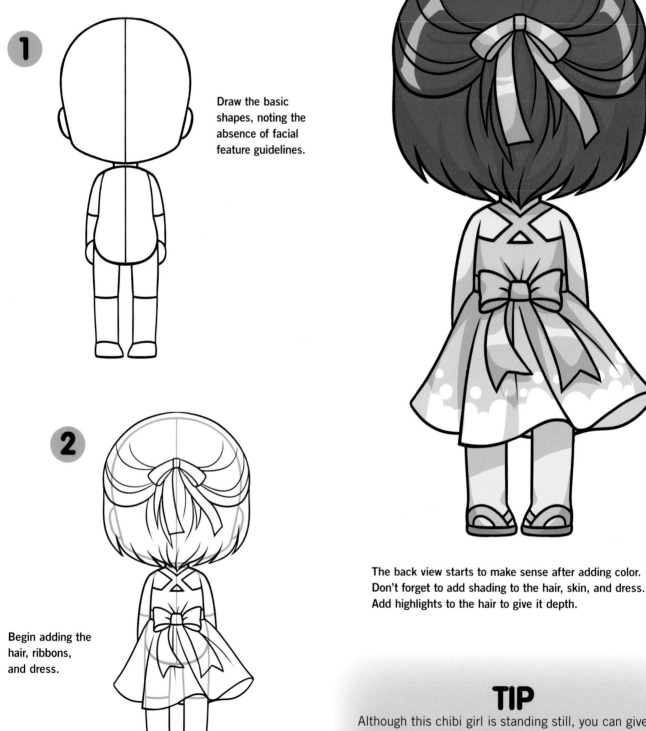

1 Draw the basic shapes, noting the absence of facial feature guidelines.

2 Begin adding the hair, ribbons, and dress.

3 The back view starts to make sense after adding color. Don't forget to add shading to the hair, skin, and dress. Add highlights to the hair to give it depth.

TIP

Although this chibi girl is standing still, you can give her pose movement with a few tricks. Notice the way the ribbons in her hair and on her dress sway a bit to the right. Her dress blows to the right, as well, which gives the illusion that she's standing outside on a breezy day.

CHIBI BODY: 3/4 VIEW

Now that you've mastered the front, side, and back views, let's sketch Sakura at a 3/4 view.

1

Draw Sakura in a frolicking pose with basic shapes and guidelines.

2

Now draw the hair, facial features, and clothes. Erase unnecessary sketch lines before moving to color.

3

Add Sakura's color, or make up your own!

READY TO PRACTICE?

Use the templates on pages 115–117 to practice drawing chibis in the front, side, and 3/4 views. You can either scan the templates to your computer and print them out, or photocopy them from the book.

SUPER-CHIBIS

Super-chibis (also called mini-chibis) look even smaller and more simplified than average ones. Check out the basic shapes that make up the front view of this super-chibi at right. The head is huge and is almost half the super-chibi's total height! The body takes up the other half, and body parts are even smaller and shorter. Super-chibis have a doll-like appearance.

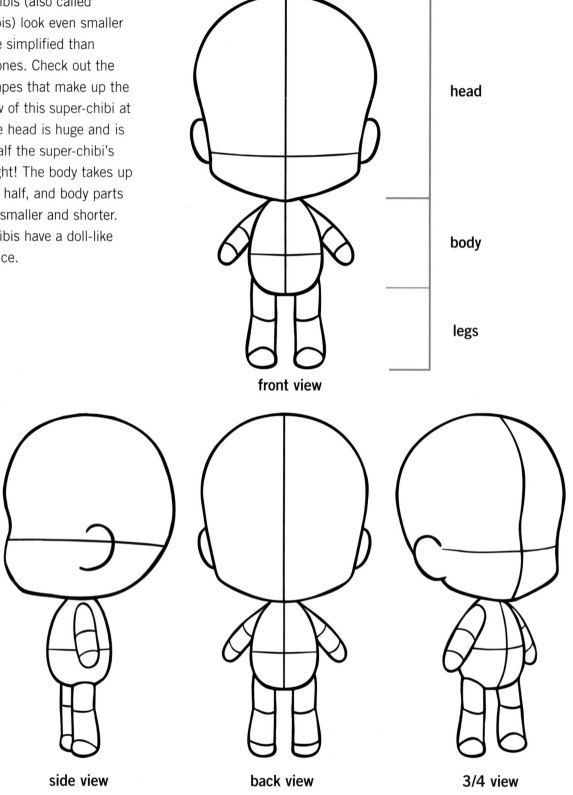

head

body

legs

front view

side view

back view

3/4 view

Above is the super-chibi from other angles. The guidelines on the face and body show which direction each form faces. Super-chibis don't typically have necks, which makes them look cuter and more compact. Legs are usually stout at the thighs, narrowing to little rounded tips. Some super-chibis don't even have elbows or knees. Some have nub-like, mitten-shaped hands, rather than fingers. Super-chibis are worlds of fun to draw—especially when you experiment!

SUPER-CHIBI BODY

Because super-chibi body parts are simplified, the hands and feet nearly meld with the arms and legs. Super-chibis typically don't have ankles and wrists either. This super-chibi doesn't have a neck, as her body is too short to accommodate one. Her mouth is large, and her huge eyes take up most of the face. Some super-chibis have noses; others do not.

Start with basic shapes and guidelines. Notice how big the head is! Her arms and legs are super short. Her hands are little nubs with tiny thumbs. Her feet are smaller and only a tad wider than her legs.

When you have the pose down, draw the details using the basic shapes as a guide. Keep things simple!

Add color, shading, and highlights to complete your artwork.

SUPER-CHIBIS IN ACTION

Super-chibi body types may be shorter and have limited motion, but they still can demonstrate tons of personality and action through their poses. This super-chibi boy appears to be running after a ball. His forward-leaning posture and exaggerated pose make the illustration all the more convincing.

Begin by sketching your basic shapes and guidelines. Add a ball as a prop, and draw its "path" line—a check mark—to show where it has bounced.

Draw a worried expression on his face, adding details over the basic shapes. See how closely the details follow the guidelines?

TIP
When adding outfits or accessories to a super-chibi, keep patterns and textures simple. Super-chibis are so small already that adding excess detail becomes distracting.

TIP
Add light-colored circles below the character to serve as shadows. This gives the drawing depth.

3

Now erase the guidelines before moving to color.

READY TO PRACTICE?
Use the templates on pages 120–121 to practice drawing super-chibis. You can either scan the templates to your computer and print them out, or photocopy them from the book.

4

Add the basic colors. Then add shading to the hair, skin, clothes, and ball. Highlights add depth and dimension to the ball. Finally, add highlights around the eyeball and then darken the pupil.

CHIBI EYES

Eyes define a chibi's personality as much as style and pose do. And they're particularly important where chibis are concerned because they're often extremely large in proportion to the face. As you review the eyes below, think about how they communicate to the viewer. What might you be able to tell about a chibi's mood just from looking at the eyes?

TRADITIONAL
- Lids and eyebrows arch upward.
- Eyeballs are oval-shaped and clear, leaving room for the pupil and the highlights.
- For boy chibis, remove the long lashes.

ALMOND-SHAPED
- Eyelids have narrow outer edges for a focused and masculine look.
- Add eyelashes or makeup for a mature, determined girl chibi.

DOE
- Long eyelashes, white highlights, and a furrowed brow communicate innocence.
- Girl chibis that are soft-spoken and kind often have doe eyes.
- Remove the eyelashes, and they work well for shy guys.

SLY
- Narrow eyes suggest complex feelings.
- The eyelids are slimmer and the eyeballs are smaller.
- Crafty characters and villains are good candidates for this eye style.
- For a demonic look, add catlike pupils and red eyeliner.

GIRLY
- Many *shoujo* (or "girl comics") and anime feature female characters with girly eyes to make characters seem ultra-feminine.
- They usually sport makeup, a star-shaped highlight, and lush eyelashes.
- Any chibi from the girl next door to a pop idol could have these eyes.

CONCAVE
- A combination of traditional and almond-shaped eyes.
- The eyeballs are squarer, and the eyelids slant down and outward.
- These eyes work for male and female chibis.
- A character with concave eyes is probably a solemn, deep thinker.

HAPPY

- Eyes close and form curved arcs.
- Characters may wear this expression when they are overjoyed or acting cheerful toward others.

WINKING

- One eye remains wide open while the other eye stays closed. It's a popular expression for happy-go-lucky characters with go-getter attitudes.

IRRITATED

- Eyelids straighten into horizontal lines and both eyeballs look to one side.
- Eyeballs are cropped at the top so the eyelids appear to cover them slightly. To enhance this annoyed look, the eyebrows should gather in the center and angle downward. Use this expression for frustrated or suspicious characters.

CLOSED/SLEEPING

- Closing both eyes with the eyelashes and the arcs of the eyelids pointing downward results in a sleeping, or closed eyes expression.
- Characters with these eyes are often pondering, wishing, or simply sleeping.

SAD

- Large and droopy with eyelids that are open but angled down toward the corners.
- Add teardrops for crying eyes.
- For a "welling up" appearance, add white shiny spots to the insides of the eyes.
- Eyebrows should angle upward where they meet and then gradually angle downward, following the arc of the eye.

SURPRISED/SHOCKED

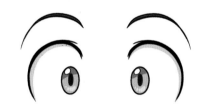

- The eyelids are large and extend outward in wide circular shapes. The irises are small, leaving a lot of white space around them.
- Arching the eyebrows higher and wider above the arc of the eyelid intensifies this expression.

EXERCISE YOUR CREATIVITY!

Practice making several expressions with your eyes in front of a mirror to become familiar with the different looks they create. Then grab a pencil and paper, and try drawing them!

CHIBI EXPRESSIONS

Facial expressions convey a character's emotions and mood. Chibi expressions tend to be highly exaggerated, often for comical effect. The combination of an over-the-top expression with a chibi's simplified style results in a wealth of character and feeling. Check out the illustrations below to see how various expressions translate between forms. And always remember that there are plenty of other ways to render each emotion.

HAPPY/CHEERFUL (NORMAL)
With closed eyes and arched eyebrows, our normal female appears to have a happy expression. The light blush on her cheeks suggests she may be shy.

HAPPY/CHEERFUL (CHIBI)
The chibi's facial features are similar to the normal figure's features, except they are closer together and sit lower on the face. The arcs of her eyelids and her smile are exaggerated.

EMBARRASSED/BASHFUL (NORMAL)
This character just ran into the boy she likes! See how her eyeballs point slightly upward? This subtle adjustment gives the girl a sense of hopefulness. Her nose and cheeks are flush.

EMBARRASSED/BASHFUL (CHIBI)
Here, the chibi's eyes are larger and rounder, although they still point upward. Her eyebrows gather at the top and slant downward. The flush covers almost all of her small face, really exaggerating the look of embarrassment. And her mouth is agape, as if she's babbling. Finally, notice the sweat drops, which are off of her face for a cute effect.

UPSET/CRYING (CHIBI)
Chibi-fying can turn even a somber moment comedic. Our girl's eyes squeeze tightly shut and spew substantial jets of water from the sides (a common style of drawing tears in Japanese anime and manga). Her eyebrows slant downward. The mouth is essentially the same shape, but grossly exaggerated. Adding sweat drops and clenched fists further illustrates that this is a chibi girl on the verge.

UPSET/CRYING (NORMAL)
Our female character's eyes are large and wet with tears. Her eyebrows slant downward in a worrisome pose, and her face is flushed. Her mouth forms an open frown, as if she's about speak before turning on the waterworks.

CONFUSED (NORMAL)

This puzzled guy's eyeballs rotate slightly toward the middle of his face, suggesting intense focus. Notice how the irises do not touch the bottoms or tops of the eyelids. His eyebrows are nearly horizontal and border on a frowning pose. His mouth is angled into a slight frown.

CONFUSED (CHIBI)

The eyes are larger and point toward the center of the character's face. They also point upward a bit to show that he's thinking. Notice how one eyebrow turns up and the other turns down, signaling confusion. This is further emphasized by the "O" shape of his mouth. Finally, question marks bouncing off his head add a finishing touch to this illustration of a truly perplexed boy.

ANGRY (NORMAL)

To convey agitation, the character's eyes narrow and point toward the center of the face. His eyebrows gather in the lower center, winging up and outward. Notice the blush concentrated on his nose and extending to his cheeks. Line dashes on his cheeks add drama, while gritting teeth show a grimace.

ANGRY (CHIBI)

Anger gets more comical in chibi form because the character appears so worked up he could explode. Notice how much more the irises of the eyes have shrunken. The eyebrows angle severely in a livid expression. The flush and dashes on the cheeks remain, and the mouth is larger and wider.

EXHAUSTED (NORMAL)

The eyes say it all: They're closed, with the arcs pointing downward. The eyebrows gather in the middle before angling down and out. His mouth is open, and he has just released a big sigh, which is shown as a small gust of air. A bead of sweat running down his cheek further emphasizes his state.

EXHAUSTED (CHIBI)

In chibi form exhausted eyes are thick, straight slits, with skin folds on the top and bottom of each eyelid. The eyebrows scrunch up near the middle, and the mouth is smaller and wider. The gust of air is bubble-shaped to look more chibi-like.

SHOCKED (NORMAL)

This girl is taken aback! Her eyes are wide and round, and the irises are tiny dots. The top and bottom eyelids are framed by high-arching eyebrows. The exaggerated gaping mouth and hunched shoulders emphasize that this character is truly floored.

SHOCKED (CHIBI)

The eyes, still framed by arched eyebrows, are two white circles, with tiny dots for the irises. Her mouth is grossly exaggerated and extends past the chin and cheeks. Additional details, such as straggling hairs, further emphasize this character's surprise. The yellow star-like icon is frequently used to indicate a flash within the mind or to suggest that something is physically jolting.

OTHER EXPRESSIONS

You've learned plenty of expressions to get you started, but there are many more to try out as you continue to draw chibis and create your own characters. Below are even more chibi expressions. Can you identify the emotion of each?

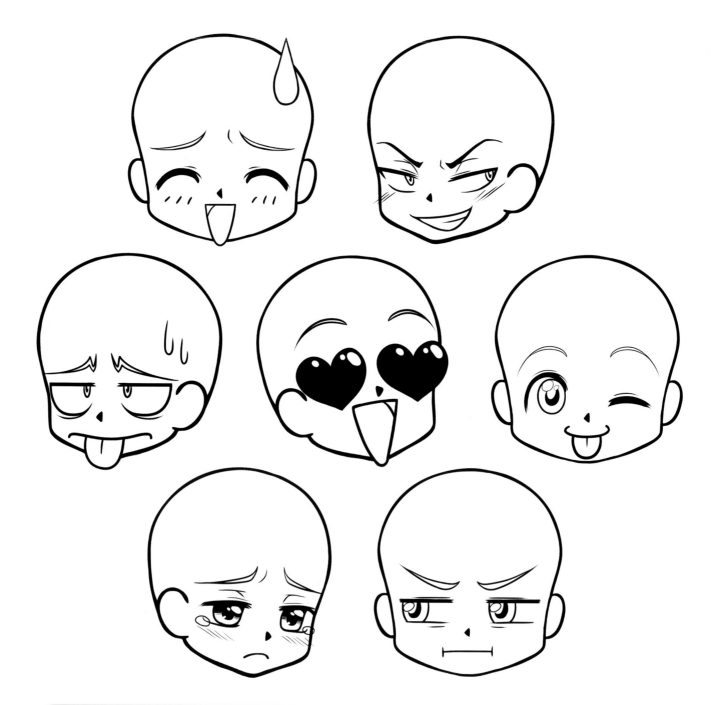

EXERCISE YOUR CREATIVITY!
Make a list of expressions, including any from this section. Next, sit in front of a mirror with a pencil and paper, and start drawing! If you get stuck, simply make the face you're trying to draw in the mirror and translate it into your drawing—it's a trick even professional artists use.

EXPRESSION TEMPLATES

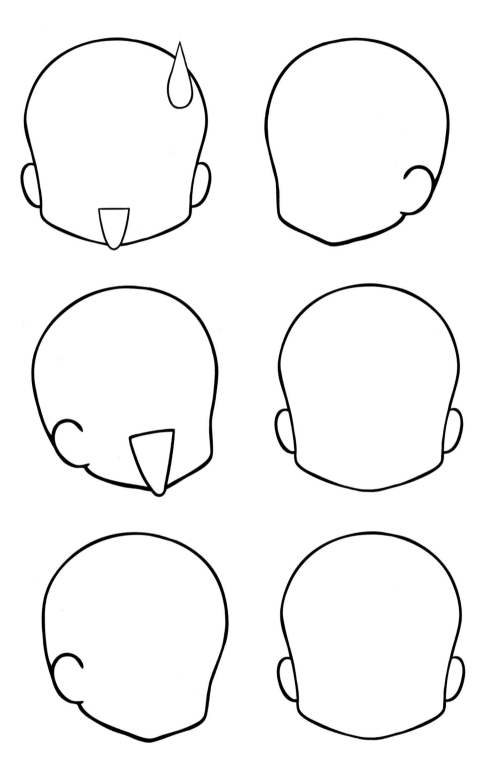

READY TO PRACTICE?
Use the templates above to practice creating your own chibi expressions. You can either scan the templates to your computer and print them out, or photocopy them from the book.

GIRL HAIRSTYLES

A hairstyle is important when developing a chibi character because a chibi's shape lacks detail. Some chibi styles are so simplified that the only distinguishing feature between characters is the hair and clothes. Drawing the right hairstyle can enhance a character's look and personality—and there are virtually no limits. Hair can be any length, style, color, or shape.

LONG, STRAIGHT The key characteristics of this traditional style are its blunt edges and straight bangs. Pair a dark color with this style for a bold statement. It's so versatile that it's ideal for almost any type of character—even some guys!

PIGTAILS There are many ways to draw pigtails and ponytails, but short pigtails are gathered high on the head. The bangs fall loosely on the forehead and clump together to form points at the tips. For added character, two little wisps of hair fall across each ear. This hairstyle is good for cheerful, fun-loving characters.

BRAIDS This character has symmetrical braids: The left and right sides mirror each other. Her braids fall past her shoulders, and her bangs divide down the middle and are tucked behind her ears. To draw less complex braids, simply sketch them as outlines, as demonstrated in the sketch at left. Characters who are shy or studious often wear braids.

LONG, WAVY This hairstyle is long and falls in random waves around the face and shoulders. The bangs are poufy, illustrated by how the hair flows forward from the widow's peak and across the face. Additional tufts of hair flank the cheeks and cover the ears, adding volume and body.

BOY HAIRSTYLES

In real life, boys' hairstyles tend to be short and not as varied as girls' styles. But because anything goes with chibis, let your imagination run free when creating boy hairstyles!

BOWL CUT Similar to the long, straight girl hairstyle, the bowl cut features bangs cut straight across the forehead and a cowlick. Geeky or nerdy characters commonly have this cut, as do quiet, reserved characters.

SPIKY This hairstyle is common in male anime and manga characters. Hair juts out in every direction in uneven and random chunks. Uneven bangs fall naturally against the forehead. You may find this unkempt hairstyle on young, active male characters and heroes. On a girl, this style signals spunk, high energy, and a slightly tomboyish personality. Works either way!

SHORT CUT This hairstyle is trimmed all the way around the head, with the longest pieces on top forming short, spiky waves. This style is typically found on "nice guy" characters or military/soldier types.

WIDOW'S PEAK WITH LONG BANGS A widow's peak is hair that grows toward the center of the forehead and forms a V. This short style sports extra-long bangs that partially cover the eyes. This style looks good on girl and boy characters.

TIP

For more ideas, flip through your favorite manga or anime to see which styles the characters are wearing.

HAIR TIPS & TRICKS

Now that you've seen a few great hairstyles for both genders, let's go over some useful tips for drawing hair. Remember that hair is just as unique as body type. Some hair is thin and light, while other hair may be thick and full. These attributes are what give hair personality, so have fun with them.

The most important factor for drawing straight hair is to use straight lines, of course! With this short, straight cut, the red arrows show the sections and outlines that should be straight. The style may vary when outside elements are at play, such as wind, or if the character is moving swiftly in one direction.

TIP

After learning to draw a variety of hairstyles, experiment by combining styles or making up your own creations!

Notice how our green-haired boy has varying lengths of hair that "sprout" in different directions. Hair grows from the crown of the head and falls downward. And the longer the hair, the heavier it is. Drawing sections of hair in different sizes and having them fall naturally is important here. The bangs form straight lines, but they also taper slightly to the side. Each section varies slightly in length, which prevents the style from looking too stiff.

This chibi girl has long blonde hair that appears to be blowing in the wind or moving as she turns her head. Long, sweeping lines suggest waves in her hair, and the pieces separate into different sections toward the tips. Drawing hair that moves in one piece and in one direction would look stiff and unnatural. Scour your favorite anime or manga for examples of how other artists draw hairstyles in wind or water.

EXERCISE YOUR CREATIVITY!
On a piece of paper, draw a variety of squiggles, zigzags, and swirls; then use those lines to create a bunch of unique hairstyles.

When drawing curly hair, remember that the hair itself doesn't change length or shape. Think of what happens to a straight ribbon when you curl it with scissors. The ribbon's length remains the same, but the ribbon appears shorter because it forms curls. Check out the sketch of the curled hair and note the red spiral arrow next to it. Can you see the direction of the arrow inside the curl? (Don't forget gravity's role!) Curls are heavy, so they don't point in all directions like spiky hair. Instead, curls gently frame the face as they flow downward. The bangs are a flattering combination of straight and curled pieces.

CHIBI HANDS

Drawing hands is one of the most challenging aspects of drawing a person. Hands help express a character's mood, but they're also complex body parts, with joints and fingers that bend and curl in many directions. It's crucial to understand their basic anatomy before drawing them. In this section, you'll learn how to "chibify" regular-sized hands—fortunately, they are much easier to draw! For example, a normal finger has three joints, whereas a chibi finger has only one or none at all. The average chibi hand is a short, chubby version of a normal hand. Some styles, such as the mitten-like hand, don't have fingers; others have fingers that are little nubs. To create a unique look, try combining two or more styles. Experiment with different methods until you find the style you like best.

normal fist

chibi fist

mitten fist

mini fist

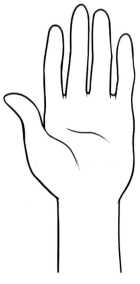

normal hand

chibi hand

mitten hand

mini hand

The peace sign is a universally known expression that's also common in anime culture.
Let's see how the peace sign looks "chibified"!

NORMAL HAND
The peace sign pose is similar to the fist, except that the index and middle fingers stick straight up to form a V.

CHIBI HAND
The chibi hand has simplified lines and shorter fingers. The last two curled fingers look fused together, and there is no thumbnail.

MITTEN HAND
The mitten hand is even more simplified. The ring and pinky fingers are part of the palm, leaving only the index and middle fingers to form the V. The thumb is indicated with a curved line, and the wrist is barely noticeable.

MINI HAND
Only a ball-shaped fist and two tiny fingers remain. The wrist disappears with only a slight bulge denoting the shape of the fist.

Now let's review a leaning hand—another common chibi character pose.

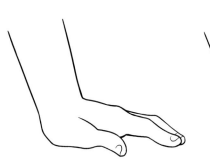   

NORMAL HAND
This side view shows a leaning hand resting on a flat surface. The arm bends upward from the wrist. In a side view, we can only see one side of the hand, the thumb, and two fingers. Try lifting your left hand in front of you at nose level; then turn it to a side view, with your fingers extended. Notice how your ring and pinky fingers hide behind the other fingers.

CHIBI HAND
In the chibi version, knuckles and joints aren't visible. Remember not to draw chibi fingers all the same length. Here, the middle finger is slightly longer than the index finger. The thumb and pinky shouldn't be longer than the middle finger.

MITTEN HAND
Here the fingers are meshed together into one shape, and the thumb is even more simplified.

MINI HAND
Here the hand is triangular shaped with a couple of lines to indicate the fingers. The bottom of the hand is almost completely straight.

CHIBI FEET

Some artists find that drawing feet is more challenging than drawing hands. For other artists, the opposite is true. Don't get discouraged if one is more challenging for you than the other. Drawing hands and feet requires practice to make them look natural. Like hands, chibi feet begin as simplified versions of normal feet. The foot shortens, toes shrink and get stubbier, and joints—even the ankle—disappear.

Below is a typical standing three-quarter pose that is common in manga and anime.

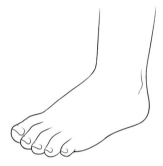
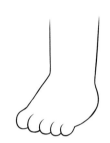

NORMAL FOOT
The normal foot is typically long, with toes that curl slightly at the joints. The toenails and ankle bone are visible, and the heel has slight definition.

CHIBI FOOT
The chibi foot is a simplified version of the normal foot. The length is shorter, the toes are more rounded, and the joints aren't visible at all. Although toenails aren't drawn here, it's a stylistic choice.

MITTEN FOOT
The mitten foot shows the smaller toes melded into one shape with only a line indicating the big toe. The ankle is also the same width as the leg and foot. Some chibi feet look like this when wearing socks.

MINI FOOT
The mini foot is more simplified and abstract. Its length is shorter, and the toes are little nubs. The ankle and leg are one form.

Now let's observe the bottom of the foot. You may see this pose when a character is about to take a step or descend stairs.

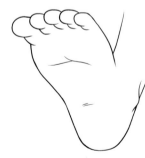

NORMAL FOOT
Although the bottom of the feet are essentially flat, sometimes drawing them is challenging. The toes curl in at the center of each toe. Additional lines show the foot's contours.

CHIBI FOOT
The bottom of the chibi foot is simplified. Toes are round and ball-shaped, and the joints are not visible. A few simple lines suggest the ball of the foot.

MITTEN FOOT
The mitten foot doesn't change much from the bottom angle.

MINI FOOT
Triangular nubs denote the toes, including the big toe, which is the same size as the others. This is a stylistic choice, so feel free to experiment.

CHIBI LEGS

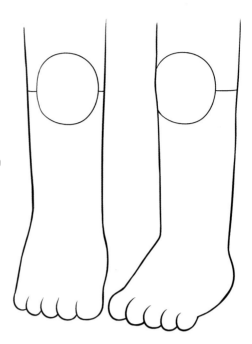

CHIBI LEGS

Average chibi feet have standard legs: short, thick with little to no muscle definition. Indents at the top of the foot and a slight curve outward at the heel help distinguish the feet from the legs.

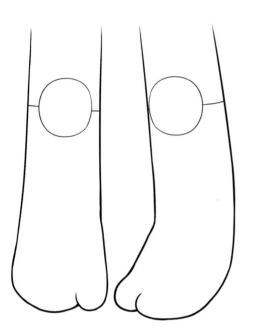

MITTEN LEGS

With mitten-style feet, legs are usually wider at the ankle and become gradually more narrow moving up the thighs. These legs have no muscle definition. The ankles are barely indicated with a slight bend at the top of the foot. Dolls and stuffed animals also have this same leg style.

TIP

Art is about experimentation, so feel free to mix and match leg and feet styles. You might even come up with a style that is uniquely yours!

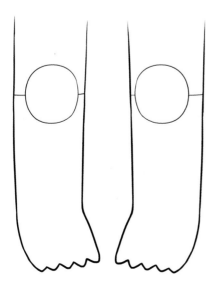

MINI LEGS

Like mitten legs, mini legs have no muscle definition because they are simplified. The width is consistent the entire length of the leg, which is straight and cylinder-like. The ankles are absorbed into the width of the legs and feet, and knees aren't rendered at all; however, keep in mind where they are if you need to bend the legs.

BASIC POSES

Because of their simplicity, chibis rely as heavily on poses to express emotions as they do on facial expressions. Knowing how to draw a variety of poses gives you far more options when conveying your characters' moods. As you know, chibis generally have fewer joints and shorter limbs, so their range of poses is a bit limited. But what you can draw (a chibi floating nebulously in space, for example) can be immensely enjoyable. Additionally, most poses can work for either gender: Both girls and boys can run, jump, kick, fly, and dance, so there aren't any strict rules. (Who likes rules, anyway?!) Let's draw our good friend Takashi in a basic standing pose.

THINKING

In this relaxed pose, this chibi sits on his knees, with the heels and calves tucked beneath his thighs. The palms rest comfortably on the legs. Perhaps he's a monk or a samurai quietly contemplating life. To draw this pose, start with very basic shapes.

FLOATING BACK

This is the *nearly* back view of a floating pose. The back of head is mostly visible, and the ear looks three-dimensional. The left arm and left leg appear farther away than the right arm and right leg. The arms seem casually raised to suggest floating. The feet also splay slightly outward, ready to land on the ground. This is a good pose for a flying character, who is landing after an excursion in the night sky.

CURIOUS

Perhaps this is a small boy looking longingly at a toy in a shop. Or maybe it's a sleepy little girl who just awoke from a nap. There are several cute elements in this profile pose. One hand dangles shyly at the side as the other barely touches the mouth. The feet are together and parallel, possibly suggesting bashfulness.

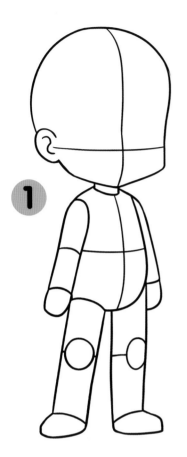

1

Start sketching the basic shapes and guidelines. Draw the arms and feet in a firm stance, but keep the body relaxed.

2

Next, draw the facial expression, which is slightly cranky in keeping with Takashi's personality. Draw the remaining details, using the guidelines to identify where to draw the clothes and hair.

3

Erase unnecessary sketch lines, and clean up your line art for color.

4

Now add shading to the hair, skin, and clothes. Darken the pupils, adding some brighter highlights to his irises to intensify his stare. Finally, give his hair a few subtle highlights.

BASIC GIRL POSES

Chibi girl poses are often free-flowing and fluid; however, the character's personality ultimately determines the pose. There is no right or wrong when choosing poses, so experiment to find the one that best fits your character.

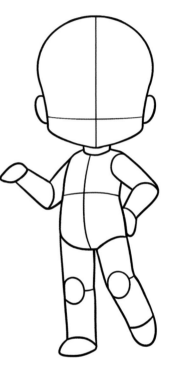

SITTING
In this pose, the chibi sits demurely, with both hands tucked in her lap. Her knees touch, her toes face each other, and her back is straight. Her head is straight, with the chin angled slightly downward, adding to the character's femininity. Notice how each body part contributes to the overall pose.

EXCITED
This chibi girl is just giddy with excitement! Her torso is straight and the vertical guidelines line up. But her mood is communicated by the position of her arms, which are bunched together in front of her chest, and her hands touching at her mouth. One leg stands firmly on the ground as the other kicks up from the knee. What does her body language say about the kind of facial expression this chibi should have?

SPEAKING
This pose could be used for a teacher or a spokesperson. Because the pose is intended to exude confidence, both the head and torso should be straight. The face looks directly at the viewer, so consider her facial expression carefully. Notice how one arm is propped on the side of her hip and the other extends outward. Finally, one leg bears most of her weight and the other shifts slightly to make the pose feel more feminine.

BASIC BOY POSES

As noted previously, male characters tend to have stronger poses that exude pride and confidence; however, many of these poses can be used for either gender, depending on the situation and personality.

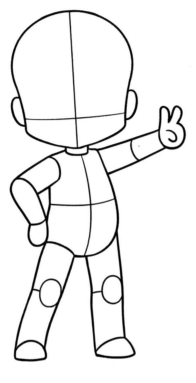

FLOATING

This pose depicts a chibi seemingly drifting in an empty space. Use it for a chibi astronaut floating in space, a deep-sea diver exploring the ocean, or as the ending point of a leaping pose. Notice how the head and torso angle toward the left, with the bottom half of the body leaning forward and the top half leaning backward. Both arms reach out to maintain balance, and both legs splay outward in preparation for the feet to land.

VICTORY

The model is clearly elated that he's come out on top, and he's making a V for victory. Perhaps he's a runner who just won the race and is posing for photos. His strong torso and head and his straight legs give his stance an air of confidence. And one arm propped on his hip suggests that he's proud of a job well done.

DETERMINED

A chibi in this pose could be ready to rumble or about to save someone from a burning building. Once again, the head and torso are erect to demonstrate confidence and bravery. The arms and legs are bent, ready to pounce into action. And one foot sits slightly behind the other to create a solid and steady pose and to add perspective to the stance.

ACTION POSES

Action poses are snapshots of a character mid movement. (Think of a photo taken two seconds after someone springs off a diving board.) Let's draw Sakura in a super-cute jumping pose that lets us know she is over-the-moon happy.

1

Begin with the basic shapes and guidelines. To achieve Sakura's cat girl pose, tuck both hands under her chin and curl her hands inward so they resemble paws. Make sure her feet are off the ground so she appears to be mid jump. Raise one leg high behind her for added charm.

2

After the basic shapes and guidelines are set, draw in the hair, facial features, clothes, and shoes.

3

Erase the guidelines, and clean up your line art for color.

4

Now add color and shading, keeping the light source in mind. The shading here is predominantly on Sakura's left, which means the light source is on her front-right side. Finally, add highlights to her hair so it appears glossy.

Take a minute to study the red line of action in each of the following poses. The line of action is an imaginary line extending from the head to the spine (or the feet). Its purpose is to provide a general idea of the direction and flow of a character's pose. Drawing the line of action first is a handy way to figure out how and where to place the arms and legs.

JUMPING
Pay attention to the way the legs, arms, and head line up with the shape of the torso to create one fluid movement throughout the body. The back is arched so the belly sticks out and the hips jut slightly forward. The head tilts up and slightly back. (You can even imagine a wide-mouthed smile on the face!) Both arms are straight and raised with open palms. Finally, each leg bends at the knees so this character appears to be jumping off the ground.

RUNNING
In this pose, the upper body angles slightly forward in the same direction the character moves, and the head tilts upward. Mimicking real-life running, the arms are in opposite positions to maintain balance. The hands are balled into fists. The left leg extends forward, with the foot nearly striking the ground. The right leg is lifted high behind the character's body.

GIGGLING
Characters in this pose can be drawn sitting on a flat surface or floating. (Imagine this character as a fairy fluttering in the sky, giggling at something she finds amusing!) In this pose, the torso is bent in at the waist. One arm is straight and extends downward. The other arm bends, with a hand touching her mouth, as though she's concealing a smile. One leg bends with the knee raised higher than the other leg to create contrast and make the image more dynamic. When a character sits on stairs, one leg rests on a higher stair than the other leg. If the character is floating/flying, having the legs differ in this way makes the pose more interesting.

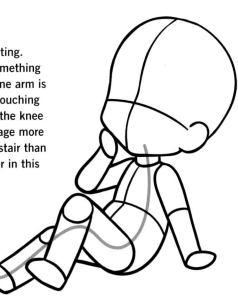

SUPERHERO

This strong line of action extends all the way from the fist in the raised arm to the toes of the extended leg. All the body parts support the action pose by lining up with each other. The left arm bends and thrusts backward, with the hand in a fist to demonstrate the character's strength. The right arm extends straight above the character's head. The left leg is straight, and the right leg bends at the knee. This chibi looks as though he/she has bounded from the ground to fly swiftly to wherever heroic deeds are needed.

WAITRESS

The top of the torso bends forward a bit. The hips jut back at a slight angle, and the head cocks to the right to give this character attitude. The right arm is bent, with the hand propped on the hip. The left arm extends slightly, as if this character is carrying a tray. This chibi is in a walking pose. The left foot kicks up, as if in a quick trot.

CHEERLEADER

Draw this pose in a front view. Because the character is jumping, the body and head are straight and aligned with each other. Both arms extend straight outward in a "Y" shape from the torso. The hands bend at the wrists; the palms are open and face upward. Both legs extend outward—the arms and legs together should make an "X" shape, and the knees bend slightly for a more natural look.

FLYING

The body parts are aligned in a straight line of action. The upper torso angles upward, following the line of the head. Notice the similarities between these arms and the arms in the running pose. The fully extended right leg continues the line of action, making the body appear long and streamlined. The left leg bends at the knee and tucks into the stomach and chest to suggest intense speed.

DANCING

The line of action indicates the flow of the body. The torso is straight and aligned with the head. The hips tilt toward the rear to support the legs. Both arms curve slightly as they lift upward in a ballet-like pose. The hands are open and extended, with palms facing inward. The left leg extends straight through the toe, which is pointed at the tip. The right leg bends at the knee and raises high behind the character—a display of a dancer's flexibility. Make sure the toes point gracefully to complete the line of the pose.

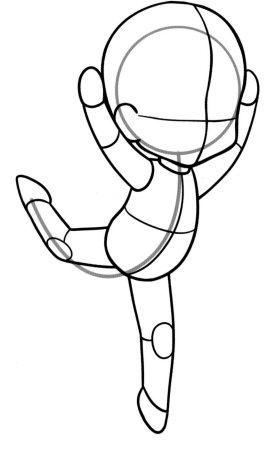

EXERCISE YOUR CREATIVITY!

Make a list of actions you do often: swim, walk the dog, jumping jacks, karate, etc. Then make the poses while someone photographs you, or you can draw yourself as you make these poses in the mirror. Designate the line of action for each, and break down the poses into basic shapes.

TUMBLING

The torso aligns with the head, but at an extreme angle to depict the sense of falling. The arms extend behind the character, as if he/she is trying to break the fall. Both legs have lost their footing, so they're flailing in front of the character. Positioning one leg closer to the body than the other makes the pose more dynamic.

BABY CHIBIS

Chibis come in all shapes, sizes, and ages, including babies, seniors, and everything in between. Remember the chibi fundamentals, and then pinpoint features that identify age, such as wrinkles, baby fat, etc.

1

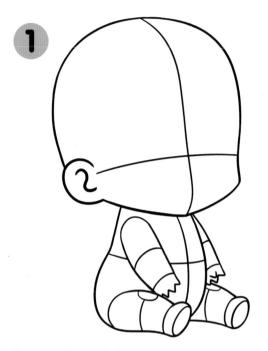

Starting with the basic shapes, draw the head so it's very round. Next, draw the body as a large potato sack shape. Make the bottom portion larger so the baby appears to be firmly planted on the ground. Babies already have short, chubby arms and legs, so just simplify them. Then add tiny hands and feet.

3

2

Give the baby large, curious eyes. Don't forget to place the features low on the face to emphasize the large forehead. Add a simple one-piece bodysuit with a tiny collar and buttons. Finally, draw a round pacifier and a little curl of hair.

Time for color! Babies have soft, delicate skin, so your colors should reflect that. Our baby has light blue eyes and wears a pink and yellow onesie. Add shading to the back of the head, body, and arms to identify the light source as coming from the front-right side. Add dark blue pupils so the eyes appear bright and curious. Also add light blush to give the baby rosy cheeks. A simple polka-dot pattern on the onesie creates subtle detail. And a small highlight on the top of the baby's forehead makes the skin look smooth and clean.

TIP

Infants have baby fat on their arms and legs, which make them even more cute. Some babies are born with lots of hair; others are born with none. Familiarize yourself with these details, so you know what to add when drawing a baby chibi.

KID CHIBIS

Now it's time to have a go at drawing a chibi kid. Pay attention to which features and characteristics define this chibi kid's age.

1

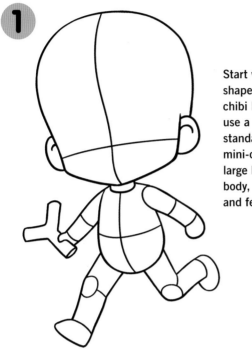

Start with the basic shapes. To make the chibi look like a kid, use a combination of standard chibi and mini-chibi features: a large head, small body, and small hands and feet.

3

Add bright, energetic colors, such as red, yellow, orange, and blue. Decorate the shirt with a smiley face, a lightning bolt, or a chibi robot for flair. Add highlights, shading, and freckles.

2

Now draw in the details, starting with the facial features. This chibi kid is a rambunctious boy, so dress him in a comfortable T-shirt, shorts, and sneakers with socks. Add a messy hairstyle and a backward baseball cap. The bandage on his knee, slingshot, and untied shoelaces tell viewers even more about this character.

TIP
Experiment giving your characters of different ages interesting personalities. How about a baby ninja or a superhero grandpa?

SENIOR CITIZEN CHIBIS

Senior citizens often have wrinkled skin, stooped posture, and gray hair. Consider these details when drawing elderly chibi characters.

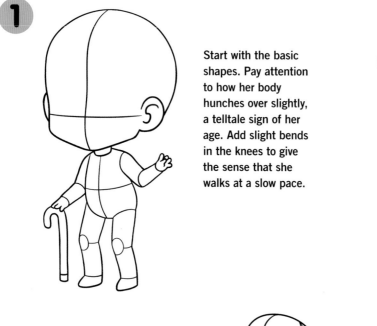

Start with the basic shapes. Pay attention to how her body hunches over slightly, a telltale sign of her age. Add slight bends in the knees to give the sense that she walks at a slow pace.

Now add the details. Granny's eyes squint slightly, and wrinkles show below her eyes and next to her mouth. Keep clothing simple and comfortable: a long, loose dress with a cardigan and slip-on shoes is age-appropriate. A traditional bun hairstyle, pearl necklace, cane, and round eyeglasses complete the look.

Add subtle colors for this character. Add highlights to the hair so it looks clean and tidy. Darken the pupils and add highlights to give her gaze more vitality. Finally, create a simple floral pattern on her skirt to spice up the final drawing.

EXERCISE YOUR CREATIVITY!
Everyday people are invaluable sources of inspiration from which to draw. You'll quickly see that not all kids are super-energetic and not all senior citizens are gray-haired. To get a sense of the differences between people of all ages, do some "people watching" the next time you are in a public place.

AGE TEMPLATES

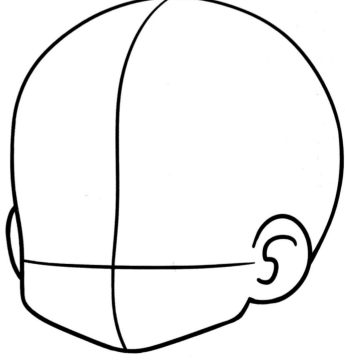

Baby

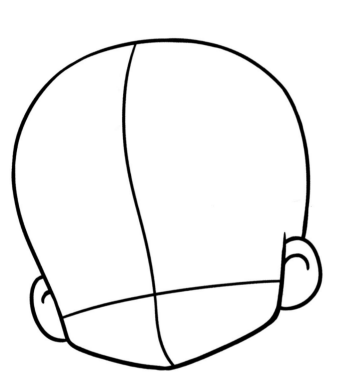

Kid

Senior Citizen

READY TO PRACTICE?
Use the templates above to practice creating chibi faces of different ages. You can either scan the templates to your computer and print them, or photocopy them from the book.

COMBINING CHIBI STYLES

As we've mentioned, there are many styles of drawing chibis. Artists utilize what they see in daily life or use a mishmash of elements to create their own styles, and you should do the same. Some artists draw super-simplified chibis, with only hair and clothing to distinguish between characters. Other artists design unique eye shapes, head shapes, body shapes, and hairstyles for each character. Try combining various characteristics and elements from previous examples to see what styles result.

Let's draw Sakura as a cross between a typical chibi and a mini-chibi. We combined a large head with a little body. She also has mini hands and feet.

Add the details, including Sakura's concave eyes, hairstyle, clothes, and accessories. Try flipping between this page and another page featuring Sakura, and note the differences in style. You'll see that many elements in this stylized drawing are simpler. We've opted to leave off Sakura's nose so she appears extra-cute and mini-chibi.

Add Sakura's colors. Add shading to her hair, skin, bows, and clothes. Then give her hair highlights. Add dark purple pupils to her eyes, as well as bright highlights to make them sparkly. Finally, add a slight blush to her cheeks.

TIP
Take a moment to compare your final drawing of Sakura with the others shown throughout the book. She's drawn differently, but she still looks like Sakura!

1 First, start with the basic shapes and guidelines. Note how large Takashi's head is compared to his body. His hands and feet are also large.

3

2

Place the eyes, following the horizontal guideline. Note that Takashi's eyebrows cover his eyelids. A few thick lines indicate his clothes. The three little marks on Takashi's cheeks, which are common on boy characters, add a blush. Although Takashi's hands and fingers are larger than previous examples, they maintain their chibiness because they're thick and round. Takashi's feet have a slight cartoony flair.

Lay down your colors to match the colors previously used for Takashi. Next, add shading to his hair, skin, clothes, and shoes. Finally, add darker pupils to his eyes to give them depth and to create a penetrating stare.

Watch out—this style of Sakura is even more simplified than the super-chibi!

1

Note Sakura's proportions: Her head is nearly half her total height! Her feet and hands are as simplified as they can be in a "peg leg" style.

3

2

This style is most interesting for the face. The eyes are two huge dots, a popular style in chibi art. The mouth looks like the number "3" if it fell on its side, which adds a bit of playfulness. The hair, clothes, and accessories are indicated by simple lines, making this version of Sakura hyper-cute and doll-like.

As in the previous Sakura style exercise, be sure to keep her colors consistent so she looks the same between illustrations. Now shade her hair, ears, skin, clothes, and bows. There are only highlights on her hair and on the bells because most of the other elements are too small to justify an additional level of color. Remember: extremely simplified styles usually work better with less detail.

Let's look at one last style with Takashi. At this stage, you should be able to recognize a few distinct features we covered earlier in the book.

1

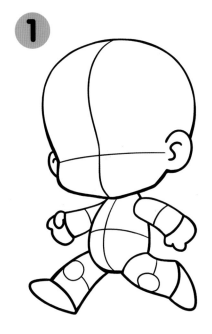

Begin with the basic shapes and guidelines. Also take note of Takashi's height: How large is his head compared to the rest of his body? The body, arms, and legs are simplified. The feet and hands are bigger than usual, but proportional to the rest of the body.

3

2

Takashi's eyes are low on his head. Now he more closely resembles a super- or mini-chibi. The clothes are drawn simply, and his mouth is open wide. Create stylized hair with rounded ends to give Takashi a doll-like appearance similar to Sakura's previous style. Use mitten-style hands.

Make sure to pick the right colors or else Takashi may not look like himself! Next, add shading to his hair, skin, and clothes. Don't overdo highlights or shading for simplified styles, or your final drawing will look busy and cluttered.

TIP

Experiment by combining a variety of chibi styles. Who knows... maybe you'll come up with your very own!

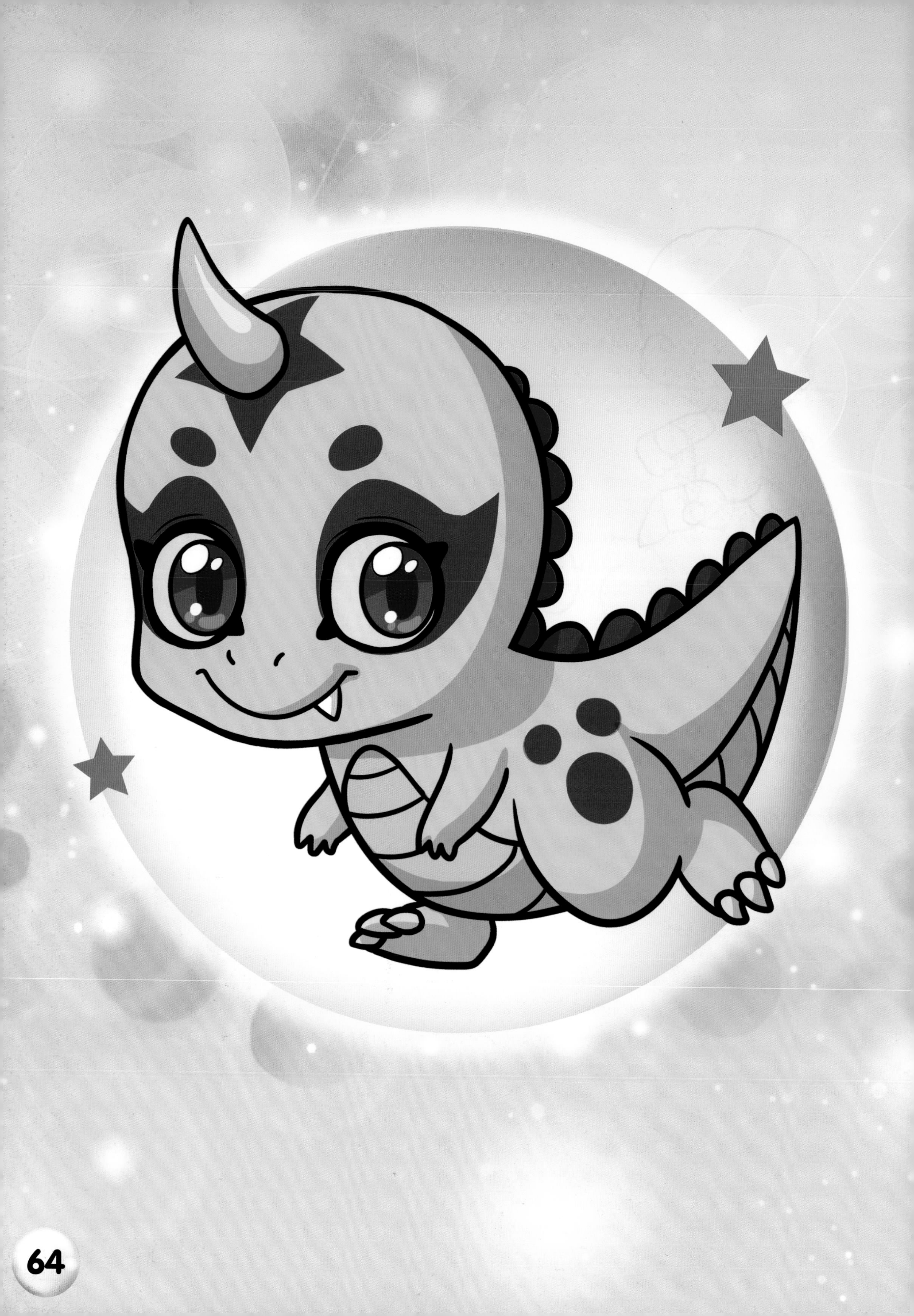

CHAPTER 2
CUTE CRITTERS

CRITTER FACES

Now that you've learned to draw "human" chibis, it's time to draw their chibi critter companions, whose features and characteristics are even more diverse! Some animals have two legs, some have four; some animals have fur, scales, or fins; some have tails, claws, wings, and beaks. The best part is that if you can draw fairy and vampire chibis, you can draw a number of critters that exist only in your imagination! Drawing chibi critters is similar to drawing other chibi characters, although the placement of the features varies among species. Most chibi animals have expressive eyes and eyebrows. They're cartoon-like, after all, so they can make all the same expressions a human chibi can make.

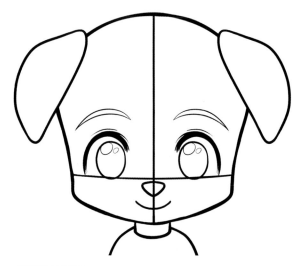

FRONT VIEW
Start with basic shapes and guidelines. Place the facial features low on the head, leaving a large forehead for extra cuteness. Then place the ears high on the head for an exaggerated look.

SIDE VIEW
Make sure the head is rounded from all angles. Then draw the nose right in front of the slightly protruding snout.

3/4 VIEW
A three-quarter view is between the front and profile views. Use face guidelines to help place the features accordingly.

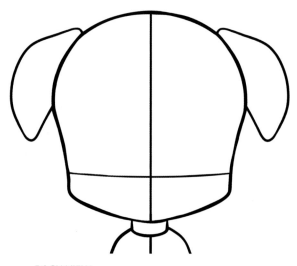

BACK VIEW
Double-check that the position of the ears is consistent with the front and profile views.

TWO-LEGGED CRITTERS

Many characters from popular cartoons, including *Tom and Jerry, Bugs Bunny,* and *Mickey Mouse,* walk on two legs and have human-like traits. Although most animals in the real-life animal kingdom are four-legged, drawing two-legged chibi critters allows for greater fun and experimentation. Proportions for a chibi two-legged critter are similar to that of a basic chibi human character. The head is larger in proportion compared to the rest of the body, which is round, oval or teardrop shaped and connects directly below the head. The upper limbs are short and stubby, and you can add little thumbs or fingers, if you like. The legs are often slightly larger around the upper thighs.

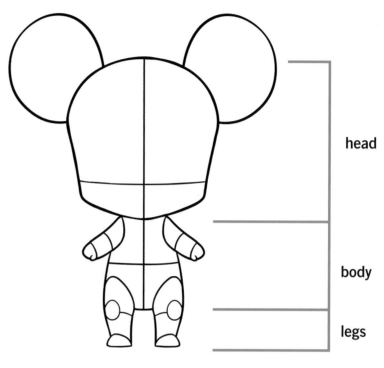

head

body

legs

front view

TIP

Feel free to experiment with different head and body sizes to see if you can create a personal two-legged critter chibi style.

side view

back view

3/4 view

FOUR-LEGGED CRITTERS

Now let's look at the body parts of a four-legged animal. Humans and animals often have overlapping body parts: eyes, head, ears, shoulders, arms, legs, thighs, and the back. Of course, there are differences. Animals, for example, have tails and muzzles. Take a look at the diagrams of a normal dog and a chibified dog. Notice that the chibi critter's head is much larger than its body, and many of the contour lines are simple. Additionally, the legs are shorter and stouter, and the paws are noticeably smaller—and very cute!

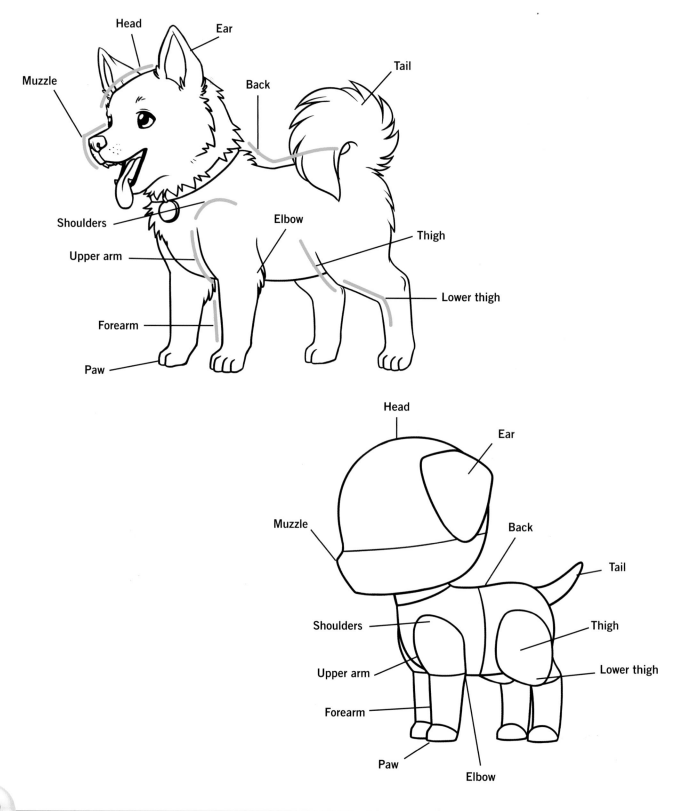

You can draw four-legged chibi critters in a variety of poses. Notice again how the shapes of the face change with each angle and that even when the angles change, the character still appears to be the same shape, height, and size from all views.

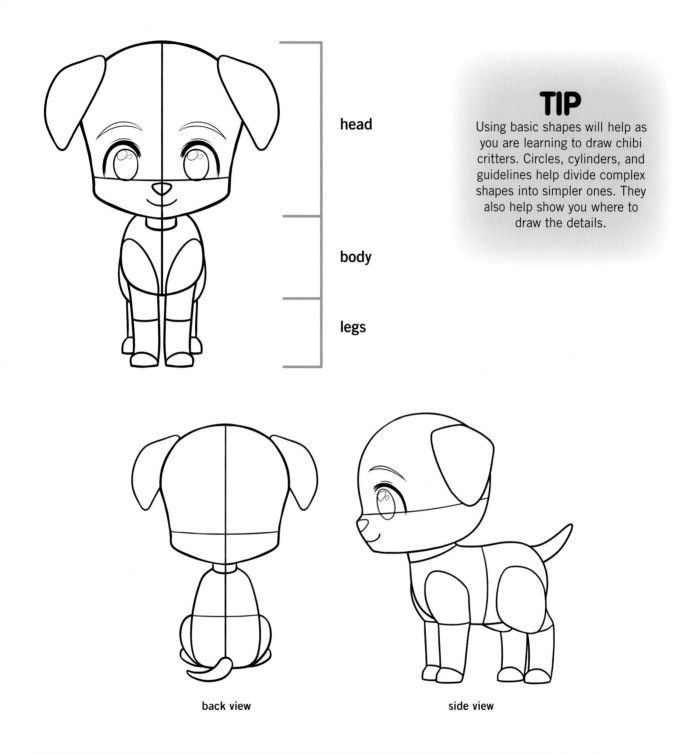

head

body

legs

TIP

Using basic shapes will help as you are learning to draw chibi critters. Circles, cylinders, and guidelines help divide complex shapes into simpler ones. They also help show you where to draw the details.

back view

side view

READY TO PRACTICE?
Use the templates on pages 122–127 to practice drawing chibi critters. You can either scan the templates to your computer and print them out, or photocopy them from the book.

CRITTER ARMS

Now let's examine the differences between critter arms and legs and human arms and legs. Animal limbs move and bend in very specific ways, so it's helpful to understand their anatomy and movements.

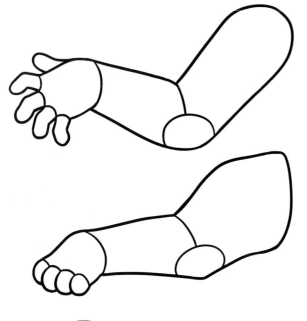

HUMAN ARM

The human arm has four major parts: the palm, fingers, forearm, and upper arm. There are joints for bending the fingers, as well as joints between the upper arm and forearm (elbow) and between the forearm and hand (wrist).

CRITTER ARM

Animal arms are similar to human arms, particularly when it comes to the joints. Because many animals walk on four legs, their upper arms tend to be larger and more muscular. Animal digits are generally much shorter than human fingers, and are packed closely together on the paw.

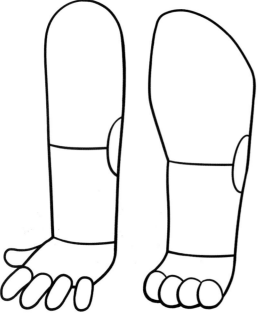

STANDING ARMS

This is what human and animal arms would look like if standing perpendicular to the ground. For the human arm, imagine a person just about to do a pushup. The animal arm shows the pose of any standing four-legged animal. Notice the similarities in the proportions and position of the primary joints. Again, the animal upper arm is larger and more muscular, and the toes are close together on the paw.

PAWS

Animals typically have four toes on top of each paw and a thumb-like digit located near the forearm. You may reduce the number of digits. Animals also have rough, hairless pads on the bottom of each digit. Render them with circular lines, adding a larger pad to the "palm."

CRITTER LEGS

When drawing animals new artists often make the mistake of drawing the front and hind legs in the same way. Study any four-legged animal's front and back legs and you'll see differences in shape and functioning parts, depending on the movement. These differences apply to human arms and legs, as well. Compare the models of human and animal back legs below. Can you identify the differences?

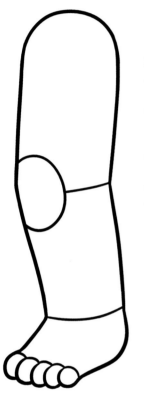

HUMAN LEG
A human leg has five primary parts: thigh, shin, calf, foot, and toes. The main leg joints include the knee and ankle, which allow the legs to bend and rotate in different directions. Toes, which are shorter than fingers, are compact.

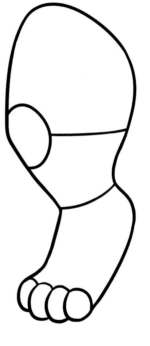

ANIMAL LEG
The animal thigh is larger, as most animals run faster than humans. The lower leg is shorter, and the foot is longer. The knee joint is pointier and juts out farther than a human knee. The ankle joint also juts out farther back. The result is an animal hind leg that forms an S shape in neutral position.

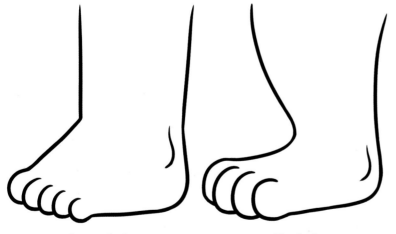

human foot   critter foot

HUMAN VS. CRITTER FOOT
In both illustrations, the foot makes contact with the ground. The image on the right is what an animal's foot would look like if it walked as a human does. Looks odd, doesn't it?

CRITTER BASIC POSES

Animals have a wide array of expressive and interesting poses, some of which are unique to specific critters. In this lesson you'll learn a few familiar poses for dogs and cats.

Dog Poses

LYING DOWN

In this basic shapes model of a dog lying down, the body is flat on the ground, with both front paws resting under the chin. The back legs fold neatly under the thighs, concealing the lower legs. Because the dog is resting, his hind foot is flat on the ground, and the tail curls neatly around the side.

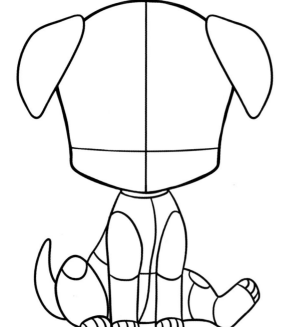

SITTING

Dogs sit down completely on their rears, with their legs curled under them or with one leg extended to the side. Both front limbs are straight and in front of the body to support the dog's weight. When drawing this pose, the head may tilt slightly to add personality.

BEGGING

For this pose, draw the torso at a forward-facing angle. The head should tilt upward, with the muzzle pointing toward whatever the dog is looking at. Raise the front paws and bend the elbows and wrists in opposite directions. The arms should appear tucked in, with the paws hanging down. Next, position the dog's weight on its hind legs by drawing the feet flat on the ground, or having him stand on his hind paws. Finally, be sure the tail appears to be in mid wag to make the dog seem excited.

Cat Poses

GROOMING

Start by drawing the body (torso) in a seated position. The back legs fold under the thighs, and the back paws peek out. Draw one front arm so it extends straight under the body to support the cat's weight. The other arm bends toward the mouth for cleaning. Tilt the head forward slightly. Draw the tail so it seems to swish back and forth, or curl it around one of the hind legs.

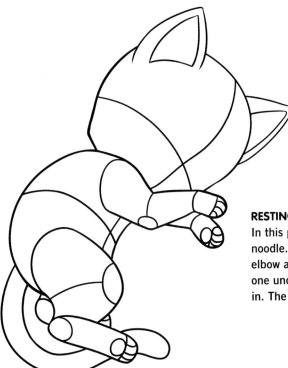

RESTING

In this pose, the head and torso curl slightly inward like a macaroni noodle. Next, draw the front legs loosely stretched out in front, with the elbow and wrist joints at a relaxed angle. For the hind legs, either tuck one under the other at slightly different angles or draw them both tucked in. The tail can rest under or around the cat's body, or in a loose curl.

STRETCHING

Draw the head angled slightly upward. Because the cat crouches so low to the ground, the torso should be angled, with the tail sticking up. Draw the front limbs stretched straight in front, with the paws extending outward. The hind legs should appear fully extended so the cat stands on his paws. Lastly, draw the tail curling forward, and angle the ears back slightly to dramatize the action.

CRITTER ACTION POSES

Critter action poses vary depending on the animal and the environment. For instance, critters that walk on two legs often have different poses than four-legged critters. Large, heavy critters may have different actions than critters with slim, agile bodies. Whether an animal is a predator or prey also figures in. Artists should invest time understanding their critter subjects, because it makes an impact on their art.

RUNNING

Most critters run on four legs. The size of the head is exaggerated and the legs narrow to tiny paws. Note how the ears appear to fly behind the dog's head, showing movement and speed. Next, visualize a line indicating the ground below the dog's legs to see how all four legs are suspended in the air. The way the toes tilt downward makes this action clearer.

ROLLING

Begin by drawing the chibi kitty's large head, exaggerated ears, small body, mitten-like paws, and chunky tail. Pay attention to the curved line of action. The head faces one direction and the body curves into a C shape, so the kitty appears to be in mid roll. Tuck both front paws under the chin and stretch the hind legs toward the sides. Finally, draw the cutest chibi kitty face possible.

HOPPING

This chibi rabbit has a large head, simplified ears, a small body, and a tail exaggerated in size and shape. The two front legs taper toward the paws, and the much larger hind legs have long simplified feet. The ears bend backward as if she's running against the wind. If you drew a line representing the ground below her body, her right front limb would barely touch the ground, and the others would be about to do the same. Be sure to draw the body angled upward, with the head lower than the body. The tail sits high on the backside, and the bottoms of both back feet face up and outward.

FRIGHTENED

Animals have specific reactions that demonstrate fear, so be aware of these differences when drawing various critters. Even without a facial expression, all the characteristics of this pose work together to convey that this is a scare-dy cat. Try to pinpoint the fundamental chibi elements and key points that give this pose movement. For an additional exercise, trace only the head, body, and legs on tracing paper, and then add the ears and tail of another feline critter. There are tigers, lions, and leopards, oh my!

SCRATCHING

Our sitting chibi dog leans slightly to his left, with his head angled so his back foot can reach it. The ears should appear to be flailing to add movement. Plant his two front paws firmly in front of his body for support. And, finally, draw the left hind leg and foot in mid scratch for a convincing pose.

DASHING

Dashing is a faster, more urgent form of running. When rabbits dash, they use their front legs and appear to be running on all four limbs. None of the four feet touches the ground. The front legs tuck close to the body, paws facing down and backward, as if they've just left the ground. The hind legs are greatly exaggerated: The thighs tuck into the body and the back feet are parallel to the body, nearly touching the head. These elements work together to heighten the intensity of the movement.

DOG

In this project you'll learn to draw the normal and chibi versions of a Shiba Inu, a breed of dog from Japan known for exhibiting fierce loyalty and affection toward their masters. *Inu* is the Japanese word for dog. *Shiba* means "brushwood" in Japanese, but it also means "small" in the old Nagano dialect. Thus, the name Shiba Inu is sometimes translated as "Little Brushwood Dog."

NORMAL DOG
Shiba Inus have trim faces with long snouts and large, pointy ears that are always erect. Their big eyes reflect their dutiful spirit. They generally have strong, stout midsections; short coats; and a distinctive tail with longer fur that curls toward the body.

Draw the large head, and add your horizontal and vertical guidelines. Now draw the basic shapes for the legs, along with guidelines indicating the joints. Note the small paws, which make the legs appear tapered.

Add the eyes, exaggerating them to look meaningful. Simplify the mouth, and add a tongue. Draw small tufts of fur in select areas. Now draw two tiny lines on each paw to identify the toes. Then give the dog a small collar with an exaggerated dog tag. Refine the details as you draw the curled tail.

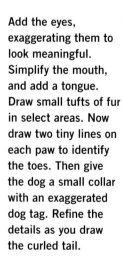

Shade and highlight time! The light source is from the upper left corner, so shadows are on the dog's left side. Add highlights to the eyes and darken the pupils. Then add gleaming highlights to the dog tag for a metallic look. Lastly, make his cheeks blush.

CAT

Where there are dogs, cats must follow! Let's practice chibifying a common tabby.

NORMAL CAT
Cats have sleek bodies, dainty paws, and tails that swish with their feelings and reflect their grace and agility. But their key feature is large, intense eyes with pupils that go from slits to big black dots. They have short snouts and long whiskers. Ears and tails vary in size and shape depending on breed.

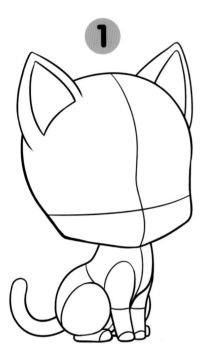

When drawing the body, try to maintain the graceful arch of the back in the sitting position. Simplify the arms and legs, and add guidelines at the joints. The paws should look especially small and delicate. Make the tail shorter and fatter for a cartoonish effect.

Add the facial features, then add tufts of fur to the inside of the ears, on the cheeks, and on the chest to imply fluffiness. Next, draw tiny slits to the front and back paws for the toes. Draw whiskers, and don't forget the collar and bell!

A feline's colors and patterns vary from cat to cat. Indicate variations in pattern with color, rather than line art.

BIRD

Birds are beautiful, interesting creatures, and have vastly different anatomy than the four-legged friends we've covered so far. In this example, you'll draw a cheerful yellow and gray cockatiel.

NORMAL BIRD

Because a bird's anatomy is so different from other animals, you must approach its chibi transformation differently. The largest part of a bird's body is its oval-shaped midsection that narrows toward the tail feathers. This cockatiel has a small head with a crest of feathers. It also has a small, hook-shaped beak with tiny nostrils. Its eyes are beady and situated toward the sides of the head. When perched, its spindly, scaly toes curl around the branch, and its wings tuck into its body.

1 Draw the basic shapes, exaggerating the head to appear large and round. Use guidelines to help maintain correct proportions. Notice the toes, which are plump and rounded, and the simple tail feathers.

2 Draw large, round eyes, and tiny eyebrows. Draw a small, simplified beak. Continue adding the details, starting with the crest. Draw a few feathers on the wings.

3 Establish your yellow, gray, and white color zones. Designate a light source and shade the appropriate areas. Make sure the shading follows the shape of the bird's head. Add darker pupils and key highlights to the eyes.

CRITTER TEMPLATES

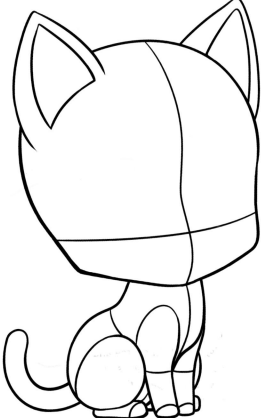

READY TO PRACTICE?
Use the templates above to practice creating your own chibi critters. You can either scan the templates to your computer and print them out, or photocopy them from the book.

CREATING FANTASY CRITTERS

Outside the realm of critters from the animal kingdom is an even larger world of critters born of your imagination: fantasy critters. Imaginary critters abound in manga and anime titles, particularly in fantasy and science-fiction stories. They often resemble real animals or a combination of animals. Some imaginary critters are a combination of inanimate objects, like a robot dog with mechanical limbs and a laser eye! Fun is the method and experimentation is key. Practice drawing the fantasy critters below. When you are done, try drawing some of your own fantasy critter creations!

FLYING BEAR
Start with an ordinary teddy bear; then add fantastical details to make him extraordinary: a purple bobble on his head; a stars and moon emblem on his forehead; large, fluffy white wings; and blue fur on his chest and feet. Perhaps this mystical creature visits sleepy children in their dreams and makes all of their wishes come true!

DINO-LIZARD
Our imaginary lizard has a dinosaur-like body similar to a Tyrannosaurus Rex. Note the chibi fundamentals: huge head, tiny arms, oversized eyes, and a chubby tail. For imaginary flair, he has unique purple markings on his forehead, eyes, and legs. Purple spikes along his back and tail add character. A single curved horn implies that, although he's cute, he can put up a fight. Always think about each specific attribute's look and function.

ROUND BIRD
This plump little bird in charming pastel colors qualifies as a super-chibi. She has an ultra-simplified body (just a circle!); huge, round eyes; a teeny beak; and simple wings, legs, and tail feathers. Her sparkly eyes suggest a sweet personality. The pretty heart on her chest further emphasizes these qualities.

1

Poko-chan has several rabbit-like attributes: big, fluffy ears; small front limbs; large hind legs; and long, flat feet. Draw the basic shapes for the head, body, limbs, ears, and tail. Use guidelines to identify the joints in the arms and legs, as well as the facial features. Simplify the contours and exaggerate!

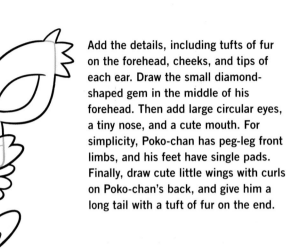

2

Add the details, including tufts of fur on the forehead, cheeks, and tips of each ear. Draw the small diamond-shaped gem in the middle of his forehead. Then add large circular eyes, a tiny nose, and a cute mouth. For simplicity, Poko-chan has peg-leg front limbs, and his feet have single pads. Finally, draw cute little wings with curls on Poko-chan's back, and give him a long tail with a tuft of fur on the end.

3

Note the light source coming from the left side. Before shading, add the lighter fur around Poko-chan's belly, nose, and mouth. Now shade his ears, head, hind legs, and feet. Add a bit of shading above the nose and below the chin for depth and dimension. Then add shading below the arms and on the wings and tail. Note the shading on Poko-chan's forehead jewel. When coloring shiny objects, using a base color, a darker shading color, and a reflective light color gives an object depth and intensity.

EXERCISE YOUR CREATIVITY!
Imaginary critters make excellent main characters in a story and even better sidekicks. For example, a girl just discovering her magical powers may need a wise critter guide. For inspiration, think of stories in which imaginary critters play major roles.

CRITTER COMBINATIONS

BUNNY-DOG-RACCOON

This silly critter has the body of a dog, the ears of a bunny, and the tail of a raccoon. He also walks on two legs, not four. Notice how his long ears match the shape of his tail and how lighter fur stripes accent both. He also sports an amber jewel on his forehead. Bright red eyes reflect his fun and fiery personality.

PURPLE PORCUPINE

A large dome-shaped body is this critter's most defining feature, followed by a row of dark purple quills on his back. Vibrant yellow emblems in interesting shapes add contrast to the fantasy-friendly purple tone. He also has a paddle-like beaver's tail and stubby flat feet. His spikes and strong tail indicate this critter might specialize in defending others.

BIRD-DRAGON

This fantasy critter has the body of a dragon and the head, beak, and feathers of a parrot. Bright red scales makes him appear bold and exotic, and his googly eyes hint at a silly personality, despite his fierce colors.

BEAR-QUAIL

Ever wonder what a bear-quail hybrid would look like? Wonder no more! Although our critter has the body shape, heavy fur, round ears, and strong limbs of a bear, it also has key quail features, such as a head plume and feather markings.

PIG-SKUNK

This critter has the chubby, oval body shape of a pig and the coloring, tail, and fur of a skunk. Little pink spots on the body, as well as rosy cheeks, give this fantastic creature even more charisma.

EXERCISE YOUR CREATIVITY!

When combining critters, start by choosing the basic body shape. Do you want your critter to be based mostly off one animal, or would you rather combine shapes from both? Then ask yourself the following questions:
1. How many legs does your critter have?
2. Does your critter fly? If so, does it use wings or does it float?
3. Does your critter have fur, scales, or fins?
4. What colors do you want your critter to be?

ANY CRITTER CAN BE CHIBI

If you were wondering whether you can draw any critter in chibi style, the answer is most definitely! Remember what defines the basic chibi style: simplification of detail and exaggeration of specific features to emphasize a certain look or characteristic. These guidelines can be applied to anything—humans, animals, and objects. Some real-life creatures may seem too scary to chibify, but as long as you follow the basic guidelines, you can chibify anything! Just select a critter's most distinctive features to exaggerate in chibi form. Here are some chibi versions of animal kingdom inhabitants not known for their cheery dispositions in real life.

LION
Our chibi lion has a large head with peg-like limbs and simplified paws. His signature mane and matching tail are rounded and cloud-like so they appear fluffy. The ears are rounded and are drawn a little larger so they don't disappear into the mane.

CROCODILE
A crocodile's menacing features include a long snout; sharp teeth; beady eyes; razor-sharp claws; and rough, scaly skin. In a chibi rendering, these features are cute, not scary. First, give the chibi croc a large bulbous head with equally large, bright, friendly eyes. Shorten the snout, but don't leave out the teeth! Also shorten the body, but add a chunky tail. To soften some features, draw the spikes on his head, back, and tail rounded instead of pointy. Lastly, simplify the limbs, and add a trio of claws to each foot.

SHARK

Let's take a look at how to turn this fierce ocean beast into a more approachable chibi character. Draw a small, round, football-shaped body. Add fins with slightly rounded tips. Next, draw the gills as two curved lines on his cheek. And give him big, friendly eyes. Among the shark's most striking features are his teeth and jaw, so give him an extra-large toothy grin. Add a few bubbles for effect.

BAT

Like other animals, bats have four limbs, but they also have large wings covered with thin flaps of skin. This unusual attribute is what you want to emphasize as you begin chibifying. To start, draw the bat with a large head in proportion to his body. Keep the ears large and simplified, and draw big, sparkly yellow eyes to make him seem less threatening. Add simple wings and feet, followed by a tuft of lighter fur on his neck and chest. Tiny fangs and a blush on his cheeks show his sweet side!

EXERCISE YOUR CREATIVITY!
Select a few animals you think are scary and try chibifying them. Determine their key features, proportions, and personalities before you start drawing.

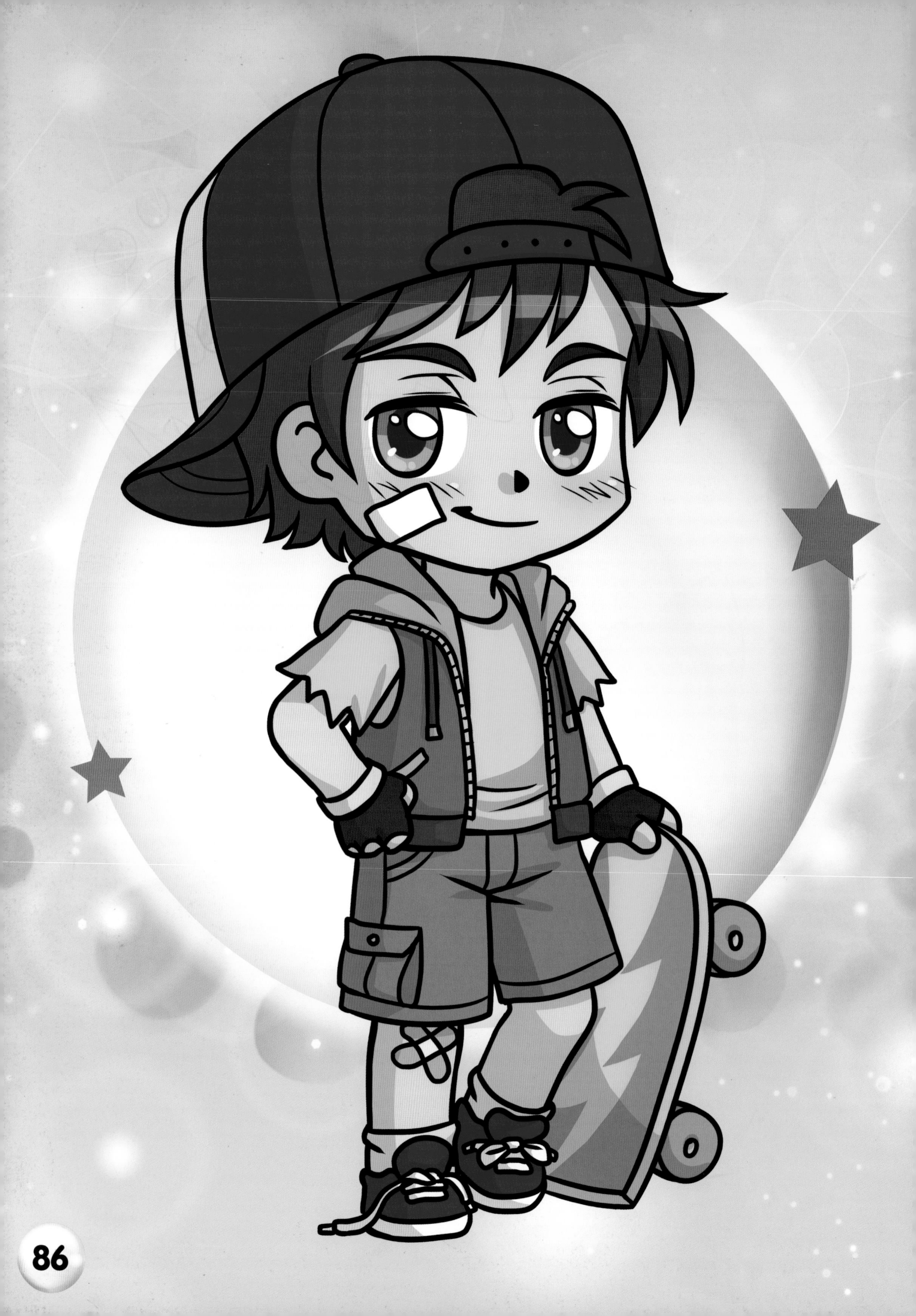

CHAPTER 3
CLOTHING & PROPS

CHIBI CLOTHING

One of the best parts of drawing chibis is creating their identities through clothing and accessories. The options are limitless, so summon your inner fashion designer and dress your chibis in a way that's as awesome as the stories surrounding them! Whether your character is a shy, studious girl in a sweater vest and knee-high socks or a rambunctious sports-loving kid in a jersey and sneakers, it's all about choosing the right ensemble to fit a character's personality. Explore patterns and decorations to enhance clothing, but be aware that using too many details may make an outfit appear busy and mismatched. Color is another key component to consider. Use a color wheel to experiment with complementary color combinations. (See "Color Basics" on page 9.) For fashion inspiration, explore magazines, the Internet, and your own closet.

Two common chibi characters include the skater boy and the bookworm girl.

SKATER BOY
Skaters are constantly moving (and falling), so dressing a skater boy in casual, tattered clothing is a good start. A green zip-up hoodie vest layered over the shirt and khaki shorts adds a sporty vibe. Other accessories include a backwards baseball cap, fingerless gloves, and red sneakers. A skateboard and a few bandages in damage-prone areas complete the look.

BOOKWORM GIRL
This little bookworm is the opposite of the skater boy in demeanor and image. Her clothes are neat, prim, and ironed to perfection. She wears a long-sleeved white blouse with a collar and a purple sweater vest in an argyle pattern. A simple tube skirt, knee-high stockings, and a pair of black Mary Janes add a bit of traditional charm. Accessories include an unadorned pink headband, huge round glasses, and a heavy book.

EXERCISE YOUR CREATIVITY!
Keep a sketchbook so you can doodle cool outfits you see every day. Use your sketchbook to experiment with different looks and patterns before diving into the final art.

TIP
Drawing an argyle pattern is easy. The pattern consists of stacked diamond shapes in alternating shades, with contrasting lines moving through the centers in "X" shapes. Try making your own color combinations and see how many argyle patterns you can come up with.

DRESSING UP

All chibi characters should have formal wear! Styles range from frilly dresses to elegant ball gowns and tuxedos to sport coats. Find inspiration for dresses and hairstyles in wedding and fashion magazines, style blogs, and movies.

FEMALE

This chibi wears a full princess-style skirt with scalloped edges and layers of shiny fabric. A long sash tied in a bow at the waist adds flair. A string of pearls, dangly pearl earrings, a dainty white corsage, and a pretty hair accessory complete the look.

MALE

When drawing a classic tuxedo remember to keep the details simple. This chibi wears a simple white button-down shirt, light gray bow tie, and pinstriped vest. Add highlights to the shoes to give them a shiny appearance.

TOPS

Let's look at a few different clothing items. This is only a small sampling of what you have to choose from so feel free to create your own chibi clothes!

RUFFLED BLOUSE

This is a darling blouse with doll-like attributes. It works well on Lolita-style characters. Short puffy sleeves make the top more cute than formal, and frilly lace trim adds pretty detail. Finally, the small polka-dot pattern makes a sweet but subtle statement.

LAYERED

This undershirt is a simple V-neck in a pink-and-white striped pattern. Layered over it is a lavender top tied at the bust, with gently flowing ruffles.

SLEEVELESS

A sleeveless top is a cute option for girls. Instead of drawing a straight hem, add a scalloped edge for more style. Scalloped lace embellishes the straps, and a cute polka-dot pattern and pink bow complete the look.

EMPIRE WAIST

An empire waist is when the dividing line of a top or dress is placed directly under the chest instead of at the waist. This yellow short-sleeved shirt with a green empire-waist top layered over it is super cute.

TIP

Layering is a really easy way to make outfits look detailed without making them overly complicated.

RAGLAN

This style of shirt is white with a collar and three-quarter sleeves in the same solid color. It's popular for activewear and sports uniforms. Add a large number to the front and back to create a jersey.

FLANNEL

An open flannel shirt layered over a solid-colored T-shirt is a great look for boys. Look closely at the pattern on this flannel: It consists of straight lines crossing each other vertically and horizontally. Easy!

PIRATE SHIRT

Who said your characters have to look modern all the time? This pirate shirt has long, billowy sleeves; a wide collar; and an open V-neck tied with a string. A plain brown sash cinches at the waist.

SHIRT AND BLAZER

For a dressy look, pair a collared shirt with a pinstriped blazer. Letting the shirtsleeves show slightly creates a nice balance of color. The handkerchief folded neatly inside the blazer pocket and the simple striped tie complete the look.

BOTTOMS

PLEATED SKIRT

This skirt's unique pleated cut leaves room for lots of experimentation. Play around with the width of each pleat, and try using different patterns, such as the argyle pattern on page 88. You can vary the length as well.

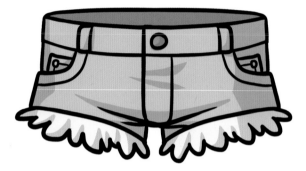

SHORT SHORTS

Draw a pair of jeans cut off at the top part of the thigh. For detail, draw in seam lines at the waist and pockets, and fray the hems. Layering these over colorful or patterned leggings creates a hip look for a modern chibi girl.

SKIRT AND SARONG

This sarong is layered over a long skirt. Pair with a cute bikini top, and your chibi character is set for a fun day at the beach!

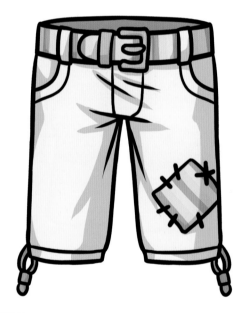

CAPRI PANTS

The length of Capri pants is about mid calf, give or take a few inches. This cute pair has a fun striped belt and matching patch. Beads adorn the drawstrings on each leg cuff. Add some sandals and a sleeveless top, and you have a fresh ensemble for a sun-loving female chibi.

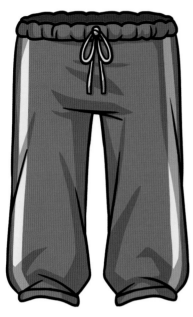

SWEATPANTS

Traditional sweatpants include a drawstring waistline, an elasticized hem at the ankle, and a stripe going down the side of each leg. When dressing your character in sweatpants, get quirky. Maybe he/she wears one pant leg rolled up higher than the other. Or perhaps your character requires an extra-fancy pair because he/she is a professional athlete.

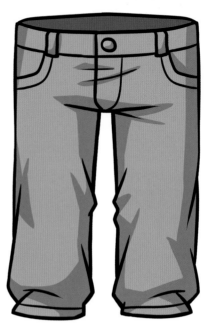

JEANS

Jeans are versatile, come in a variety of cuts and colors, and are great for either gender! They're also fun to draw because of the many details you can add, like seams, belt loops, and buttons.

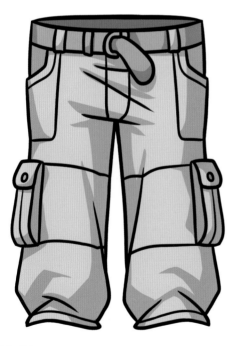

"CAMO" SHORTS

These camo (short for camouflage) shorts are longer than typical shorts, with hems that fall right above the knee. Like with jeans, draw in seam lines at the waist, on the hems of the legs, and on the pockets. Be sure to add some roomy pockets on each side so they're as utilitarian as they are stylish.

CARGO PANTS

Cargo pants come in a wide range of colors and have pockets on the side, rear, and on the legs. Some also include a belt. Make sure not to draw cargo pants too form-fitting. They are meant to be baggy.

EXERCISE YOUR CREATIVITY!

Pair some of the tops from the previous section with some of the bottoms above. Don't forget to dig through your own closet in search of other styles that might suit your chibi characters.

OUTERWEAR

WINTER COAT
The waist disappears when chibifying this chilly weather coat, and the torso assumes a bell shape. The sleeves bulge in the center, to make the jacket appear extra thick. Other details include seams on the cuffs, hemlines, and side pockets.

HOODIE
The zipper makes this casual, lightweight jacket enjoyable to draw. You can choose from a variety of styles and vary the width of the zipper itself. Like the winter coat, the chibi version of this hoodie features a bell-shaped torso. The sleeves puff out slightly, and gather at the wrists. Add dangling drawstrings at the top!

TRENCH COAT

A trench coat cut is typically double-breasted, with a broad collar and a belt or sash that ties around the waist. Try giving this coat a slightly subtler bell-shaped torso, taking the belted waist into account. Don't think you're restricted to the beige color. Bright yellow, red, and black are equally acceptable.

TIP
Always start with basic shapes and remember to keep lines simple.

PARKA

Parkas are thick, hooded jackets often lined with faux fur for staying warm in frosty temperatures. They come in a variety of colors and styles, with features including extra-warm down, heavy cotton, and round and hook/claw buttons.

FOOTWEAR

The level of difficulty when drawing shoes on your characters depends on which chibi style you're using and the size of the feet. In any case, simplification is key: Identify the basic shapes and lines in the type of shoe you want to draw, and then add the details. Let's examine a few common shoe types drawn in "normal" and chibi sizes. Drawing the shape of the feet first gives you guidelines to work with when you "wrap" the shoes around them.

SNEAKERS
Sneakers come in all shapes, sizes, and patterns. Note the difference between the normal and chibi forms. Chibi shoes are simplified and compact.

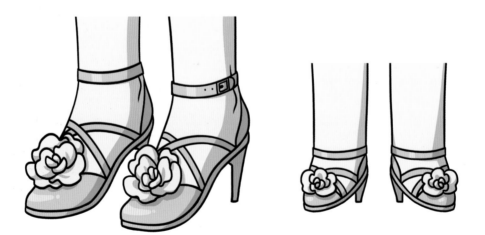

HIGH HEELS
Heels are sometimes difficult to draw in normal form because the heel of the foot is raised and there are more angles to consider. This is where drawing basic shapes and guidelines really helps! Notice the difference in detail between the normal and chibi heels. Also notice how the heel height changes between the normal and chibi versions. Although much shorter, a tiny wedge under each shoe still implies the chibi is wearing heels. The arch between the heel and toes is absent in the chibi version.

WINTER BOOTS

Because boot styles are sometimes chunky, boot-wearing chibi feet may appear chunky too. That's okay! Let the exaggerated feet round out the shape of your character. In the chibi version, feet are short and chubby. Details like fabric wrinkles disappear. Also, there is only one dangling tassle.

SANDALS

The length of the foot is shortened in the chibi sandals, and the length of the strap is shorter also. To review drawing feet, turn to page 46.

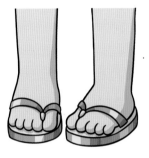

STEEL-TOED BOOTS

This is rugged footwear for tough characters, especially serious, dark, fighter types. As always, length is the most dramatic change, but there is a lot to simplify in the chibi version. Notice that there are two belts instead of three. The zipper remains, but it's wider in the chibi version. The steel-toe tip shrinks, but the studs get larger, and there are only four, rather than five, on each foot. Finally, the grooves on the soles of the boots are closer together in the chibi version, due to reduced foot length.

EXERCISE YOUR CREATIVITY!

A great way to practice drawing shoes is to draw your own! Try sketching them in a normal-sized style first. Then draw them chibi style.

HATS

Hats are tons of fun to add to chibi characters. Try not to let hats overpower the image; the key is to find balance. When choosing a style, consider your chibi's environment—and, of course, personality.

BASEBALL CAP
Characters of either gender can wear this hat forward, backward, sideways, or tilted for different effects. When drawing it in chibi style, make the brim a bit shorter, or else it'll appear too long compared to your chibi's face. For a customized look, create a unique emblem for the front.

KNIT CAP
This cozy winter accessory also works on both genders, and it looks great in solid colors or fun patterns. As you sketch, experiment with proportions: the size of the pom-poms and the length of the ear flaps, for example. The key to drawing these caps is to keep the lines around the edges smooth and curved.

COWBOY HAT
Drawing a sheriff or ranch hand? A cowboy hat is a must. Study a cowboy hat, and you'll see how the brim slopes down in the front and back, and then curls up on the sides. To make the hat more feminine, simply change the colors and add a flower or ribbon.

SUN HAT
For this casual, feminine hat, draw a round dome for the top and a brim that extends out and slopes down at the sides. Creating the woven straw texture is easy. A simple crisscross pattern is all you need.

PAGEBOY CAP
The top of this cap is big and loose; it slopes over the edges when worn. Draw basic shapes for a baseball cap, and then draw the cap portion as if you're drawing a deflated balloon.

BAGS

Bags and purses speak volumes about a character. A student isn't complete without a backpack, and a lone warrior must travel with his humble satchel of a few worldly goods.

BACKPACK

This plump little backpack features two compartments. Have fun decorating yours with zippers and seams, but keep things simple. Challenge yourself to draw school backpacks, camping backpacks, laptop bags, or whatever inspires you.

FANNY PACK

To create this travel-friendly bag, begin by drawing a belt. Next, attach a small pouch. The pouch doesn't always have to be in front; it can be on either side or even on the back of the character. Add pockets and zippers as needed.

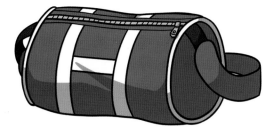

DUFFEL BAG

A duffel bag is perfect for sporty chibi characters, including boxers, karate students, cheerleaders, and gymnasts. Draw a cylindrical shape for the base, and then decorate it with seam lines, zippers, and a strap.

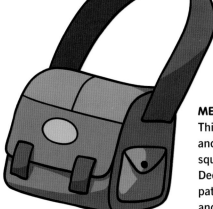

MESSENGER BAG

This bag comes in all shapes and sizes. Start with a basic square, but round the edges. Decorate it with seam lines, patches, zippers, pockets, and straps. Make it girly with butterfly patches, or add a keychain charm hanging from one of the straps.

PURSE

Purse styles range from clutch bags to hobo bags. Our example is a pocketbook purse, which is usually square-shaped with a long, thin strap attached with loops or buckles. Definitely try out different patterns and embellishments!

CHIBI PROPS

The sky's the limit when it comes to chibi props. Fantasy warrior characters may need swords, magical staffs, armor, and shields. A chibi athlete could use baseballs, hockey sticks, or tennis racquets. Then there are every-day objects like flowers, brooms, and video game controllers. Take a look at a few random props below, which we drew in both normal and chibi style.

SWORD
The first obvious difference between the two swords is how much shorter and wider the chibi version is. The blade is still pointed, but the shape of the sword is simplified and exaggerated. The hilt and handle are also shortened, and the handle gets fatter toward the end, rather than staying the same width.

FLOWER
The chibi daisy only has five petals, and its size and shape are exaggerated. The flower's center is a smooth circle and the stem is shorter and wider. When drawing other detail-rich flowers, like roses, in chibi style, exaggerate key features that capture the essence of the flower.

BROOM
The chibi broom is shorter and fatter than the normal broom. Its broomstick is slightly uneven compared to the normal version's straight, symmetrical broomstick. And the straw has rounded edges.

MAGICAL STAFF
Any fantasy buff is familiar with magical staffs and wands. Our design is fairly common: It has a long wooden base with a gnarled top, and holds a gemstone. The chibi version is much shorter and fatter than the normal version, and many bumps and grooves are simplified. But pay close attention to the proportions. The jeweled grip piece is nearly the same size as its normal counterpart, although the chibi stick is shorter. Exaggerating the size of the grip (the focal point of the staff) makes the chibi version appear compact and cartoonish.

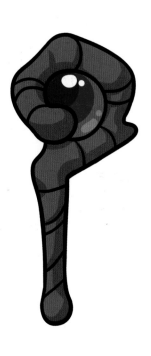

EXERCISE YOUR CREATIVITY!
Collect a few objects around your house, and try drawing them in normal and chibi forms. An umbrella, a frying pan, or even a cell phone will do.

FURNITURE

As you become comfortable drawing in your own chibi style, you may want to create settings and furnishings for your characters. Settings make your art interesting and help tell stories about the characters. When drawing inanimate objects, you still identify and draw the basic shapes. Visualize which details to simplify and which to exaggerate.

NORMAL CHAIR
First, identify the basic shapes. What guidelines would you draw before adding details to this chair?

CHIBI CHAIR
The chibi chair is smaller and chunkier, and it resembles a child's toy chair. The details are simplified. Notice how much the thickness of the chair has been exaggerated.

NORMAL BED
The main part of the bed, the mattress, is a long rectangular shape. The bed frames are also rectangular, with rounded edges in the center. The pillow is a flattened oval-shaped cylinder.

NORMAL TELEVISION
This "old school" T.V. is drawn in front view, but try drawing it in side and back views.

CHIBI TELEVISION
The chibi T.V. has rounded corners and bulging sides. It is slightly wider on top, with a wacky zigzag antenna.

CHIBI BED
The chibi bed is shorter and stouter. The pillow is simplified and is drawn to appear fluffier. The bed frame is also simplified and thickened. See how the sides slant outward at the top? This is a stylistic choice to make the bed look more cartoonish. Exaggerating the size of the balls adorning the frame serves the same purpose.

NORMAL LAMP
This lamp's basic shapes include a long cylindrical tube for the stand, a flat, coin-shaped cylinder for the base, and a cone-shaped cylinder for the lampshade.

CHIBI LAMP
The lamp's chibi transformation is as simple as making it shorter and fatter, especially the stand and base. The sides on the lampshade curve in for a cartoonish look. Finally, exaggerate the chain so the ball links are fatter.

NORMAL COUCH
The couch is a rectangular shape with two smaller rectangular shapes (with rounded tops) forming the arms.

CHIBI COUCH
The back of the couch and the arms are more rounded. The couch is thicker and slants outward for a cartoonish effect. Notice how the seat cushions appear uneven. The pillows are fluffier to make them cuter.

NORMAL SCHOOL DESK
The shape is a rectangular cube. The legs are long metal poles, with cross pole supports in the middle. Can you draw this desk from other angles? Or better yet, can you add a chair behind it?

CHIBI SCHOOL DESK
In chibi style, the top of the desk is thicker and the sides are angled. The legs and horizontal support are also thicker and rounded. Challenge yourself to draw a chibi chair behind this desk, with a chibi character sitting in it.

NORMAL DRESSER
The top of the dresser angles inward and gradually gets wider on the bottom edges. It also has two drawers with knobs. What kind of stuff would be on top of the dresser?

CHIBI DRESSER
Like in previous examples, begin by distorting the appearance, making the dresser wider at the top and narrower at the bottom. Notice how the top gets thicker. Now, simplify the details by drawing only one knob on each drawer.

CHIBI FOOD

Chibi food is enjoyable to draw. Think of the possibilities: a chibi girl in roller skates eating a popsicle or a dashing young chibi waiter serving a tray of goodies. Remember to focus on the primary details of your subject and emphasize them, while omitting unnecessary details. As always, think "cute" and "plump."

Delicious sweet confections like cakes, cookies, tarts, and tea are tons of fun to draw in chibi style. After being simplified, an elaborately decorated cake becomes a plump cartoonish shape with exaggerated strawberries and whipped cream. Although the teacup's shape also gets simplified, you can still add intricate detail to the side and saucer for a dash of elegance. Cookies are super easy to draw, as they're simple already. Cupcakes frosted with whipped cream and covered in colorful sprinkles add whimsy to the spread.

There are many ways to interpret breakfast depending on where in the world your characters live. One popular morning meal is a fried egg atop a slice of toast. Riceballs are a common breakfast in anime and manga. Start by drawing a rounded triangular shape as the base, adding texture around the contours so it resembles rice. Then draw a small seaweed strip on the bottom. An "Octopus" sausage is a tiny hot dog with one end cut to mimic tentacles. They're a staple in bento (lunch boxes) in Japan.

Fast food joints: the ideal meeting places for hungry young chibi characters. To draw a burger, begin with round, basic shapes to get the correct proportions. Draw in each detail, including the top bun (don't forget the sesame seeds!), lettuce, patty, cheese, and bottom bun. Draw a cylindrical shape for the drink. Add a straw and a design to the cup. Draw a French fry carton and rectangular shapes for the fries.

For the sundae, use long oval shapes for the glass and ice cream. Then draw another loose oval guideline for the whipped cream and cherry. For the ice cream cone, sketch two circular shapes for the two scoops of ice cream and a triangular guideline for the cone. Next, add scalloped edges to the bottom of each scoop and a little drip on the top scoop. Draw a crisscross pattern on the cone to add texture. Top the ice cream with fudge, nuts, and a cherry.

For the banana split, add loose basic shapes for the bananas and three circular shapes for the ice cream scoops. Sketch in the whipped cream and cherry.

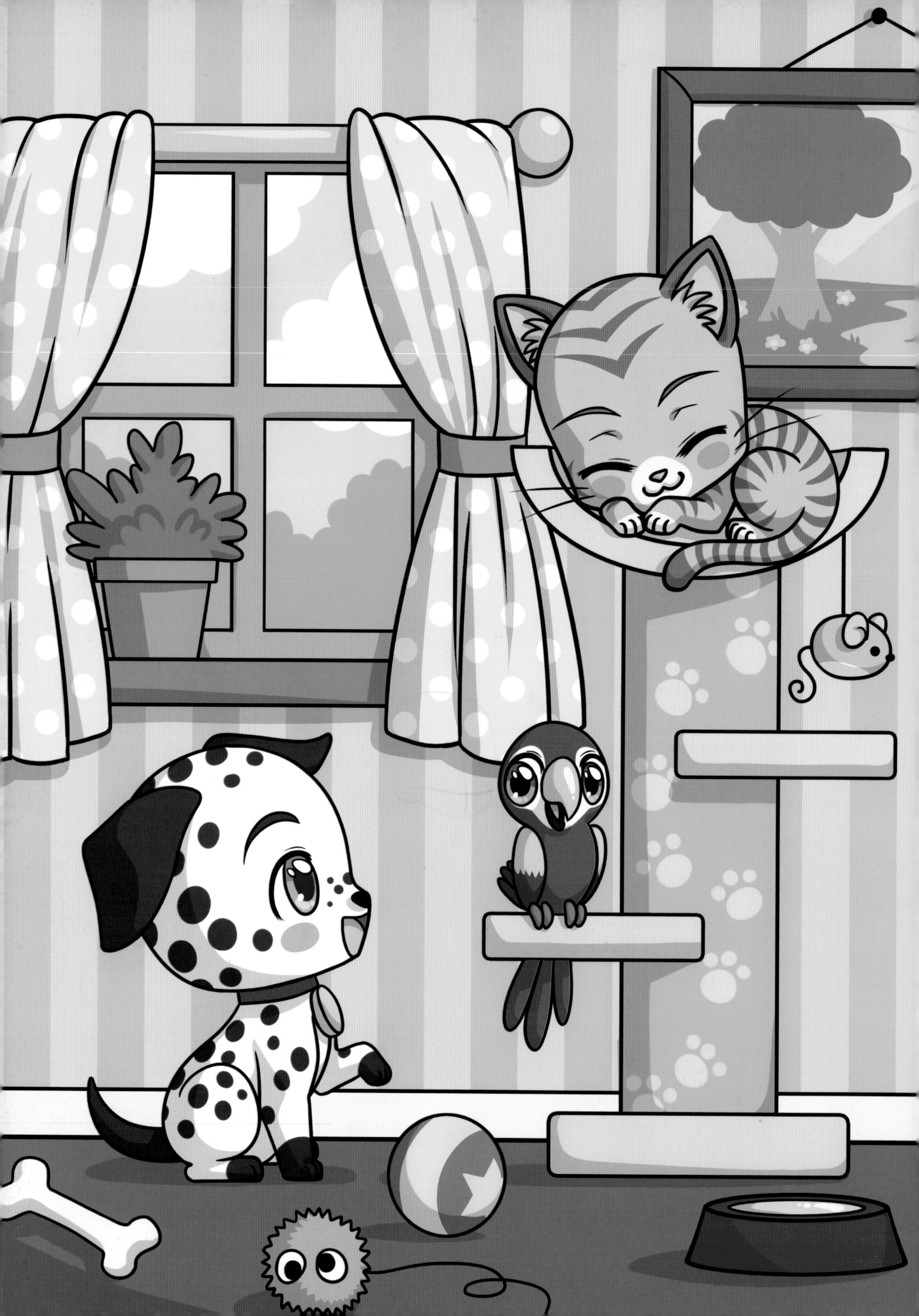

CHAPTER 4

BRINGING IT ALL TOGETHER

CHIBIS & ENVIRONMENTS

Now it's time to apply everything you've learned to draw a chibi scene. Start with basic shapes to plan your drawing. Then add one thing at a time. Some artists start with characters; others start with objects. Take your time, and experiment to see what works for you.

STEP ONE Starting with basic shapes and guidelines is particularly important when drawing a scenic illustration as large and detailed as this one. Know what kind of composition you want for your drawing before you begin. Should the characters be closer or farther away from the viewer? Where are they sitting? What's in the foreground and background? How much depth can you see in the distance? Loosely sketching basic shapes also saves time. You wouldn't want to draw an overly detailed tree only to have to erase it a few minutes later.

STEP TWO In this step, draw in your details. If you're uncomfortable drawing environments, try drawing the characters first. Decide what they're wearing and holding, and what kind of expressions they have. After you finish the characters, tackle other details. Some artists work in "layers"—that is, they draw things that are closest to or overlap with what they drew first. After characters, draw the details of the picnic basket, as well as the jars and plates. After that, draw the details of the dog, bicycle, tree, and squirrel. Such details as the flowers, grass, bushes, and mountain landscape are farthest from your starting point, so draw those last.

STEP THREE Coloring an illustration of this size and detail may seem daunting, but taking things one step at a time and planning ahead are especially useful as this stage. Start by choosing your light source, which will define the placement of shadows. Also think about what time of day it is, because it affects how you'll color your illustration. Simplification is still important. Objects that are farther away are more faded and less detailed. You don't want the mountain range in the distance to be more detailed than the characters, or your illustration will appear cluttered. Identify the main subject(s) of your image, and make them the focal point by clearly defining their details.

CONCLUSION

Congratulations! You have officially graduated from our "course" on how to draw chibis. Now it's time to venture into the world of chibi on your own, and continue exploring the things that interest you. Fear not—you have all the tips, tricks, and knowledge from this book, and you can always refer back to them if you get stuck. In the meantime, we leave you with some final words of advice and encouragement.

Practice and persevere.

All artists—even the pros—have to practice. If you sometimes feel as though you're ages away from a particular goal, remember that practice and perseverance never fail to teach you new things. When you find yourself struggling with a particular pose, practice it with a friend until you understand it. If you have trouble drawing folds in cloth, draw them over and over! Your hard work will pay off when you finally draw the most amazing folds in the cape of your newly created superhero character.

Challenge yourself.

Artists who often step out of their comfort zones usually walk away with immense knowledge and experience. After you've drawn a bunch of characters without backgrounds, try a background for your next project. Try drawing a character from the back or three-quarter view if you've been drawing that character only from the front view. Draw complicated hand gestures or feet. Always push yourself and try drawing things you've never attempted before so you can "level-up" as an artist.

Be open-minded.

Throughout your journey as an artist, you may run into people (who may or may not be artists themselves) who will say positive or negative things about your art. This happens to everyone, even the pros. It's important to remain open-minded: Learn how to identify the constructive feedback that will help you grow as an artist, and separate it from the negative feedback that brings you down. And always follow your instincts.

Have fun.

Drawing shouldn't be a chore, even if you land yourself an awesome art job. It's important to enjoy producing art, and if you do, it'll show in your work.

Sakura, Takashi, and Poke-chan say "GANBATTE!"*

Ganbatte is an encouraging cheer in Japanese. It means, "Good luck!" or "Do your best!"

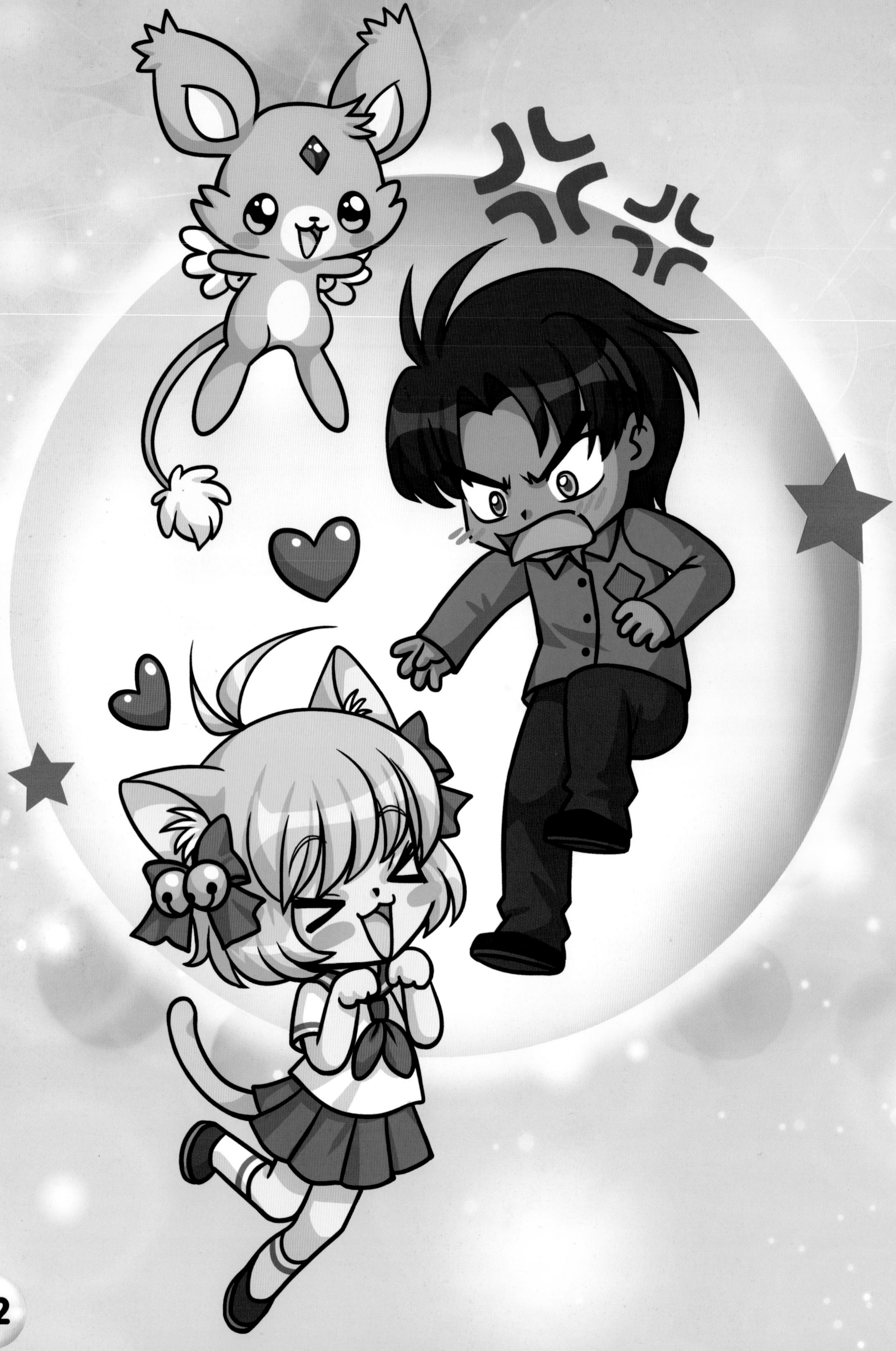

CHAPTER 5
TEMPLATES

CHIBI HEAD

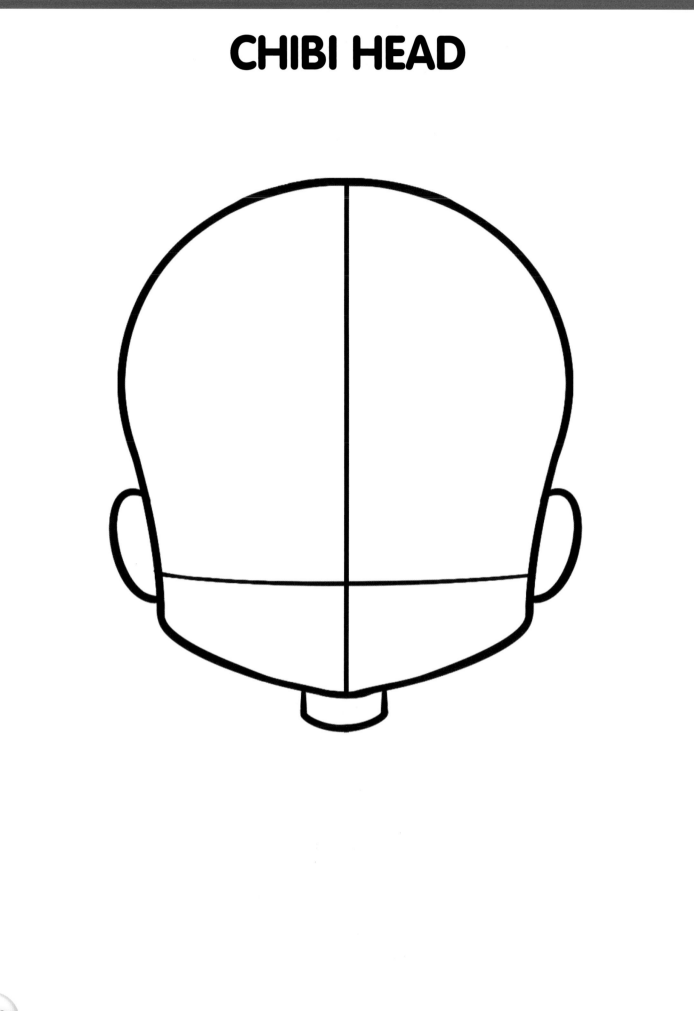

CHIBI FRONT VIEW

CHIBI SIDE VIEW

CHIBI 3/4 VIEW

CHIBI RUNNING

CHIBI JUMPING

SUPER-CHIBI FRONT VIEW

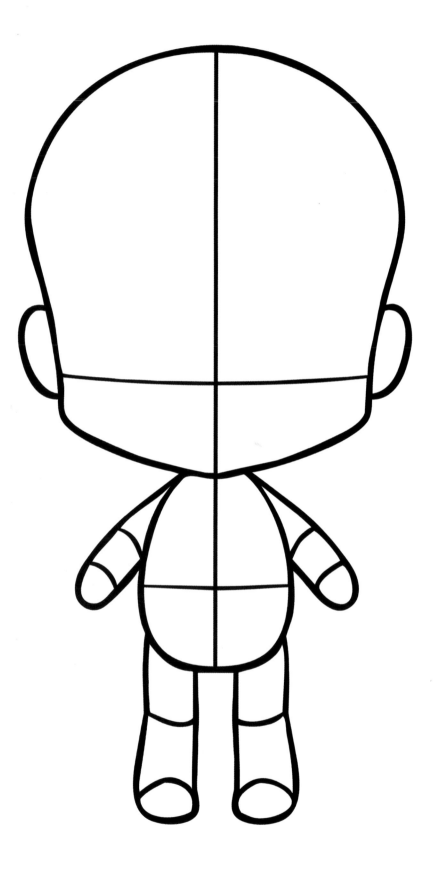

SUPER-CHIBI ACTION POSE

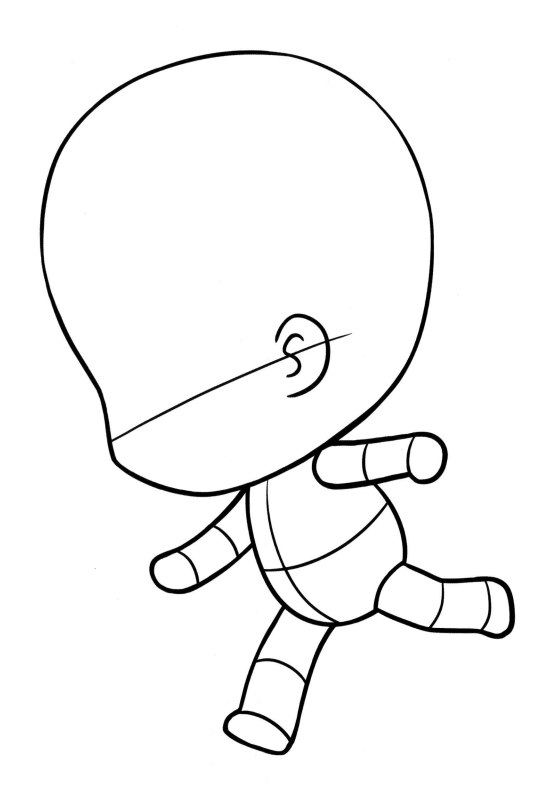

TWO-LEGGED CRITTER FRONT VIEW

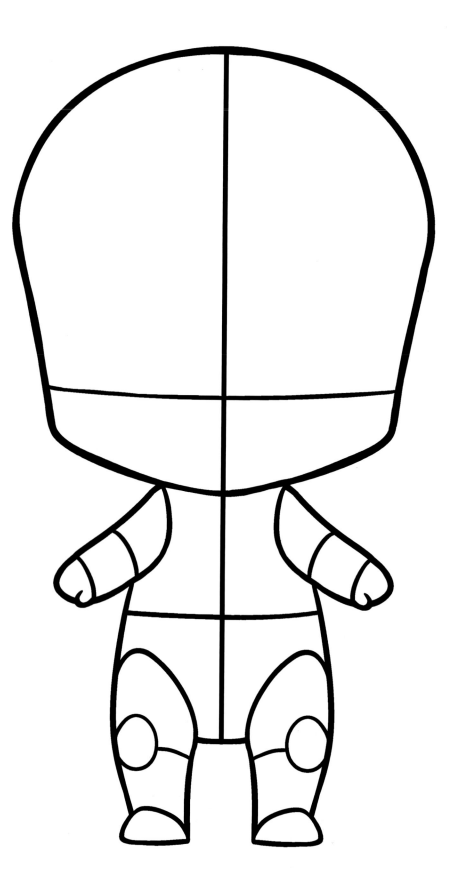

TWO-LEGGED CRITTER BACK VIEW

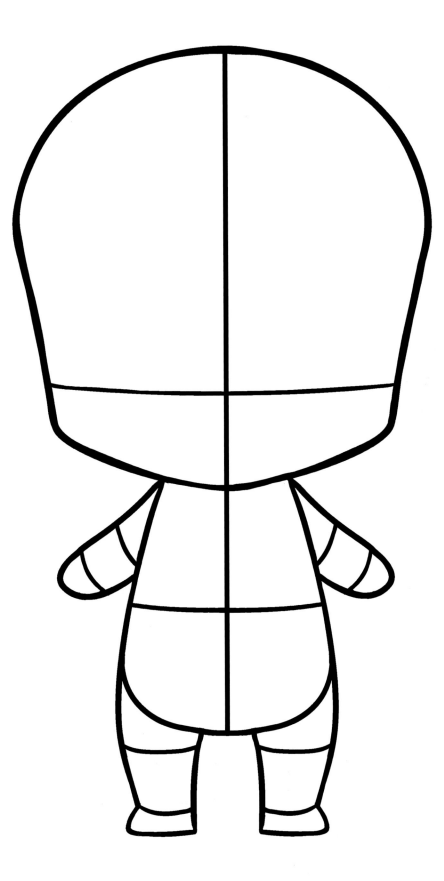

TWO-LEGGED CRITTER SIDE VIEW

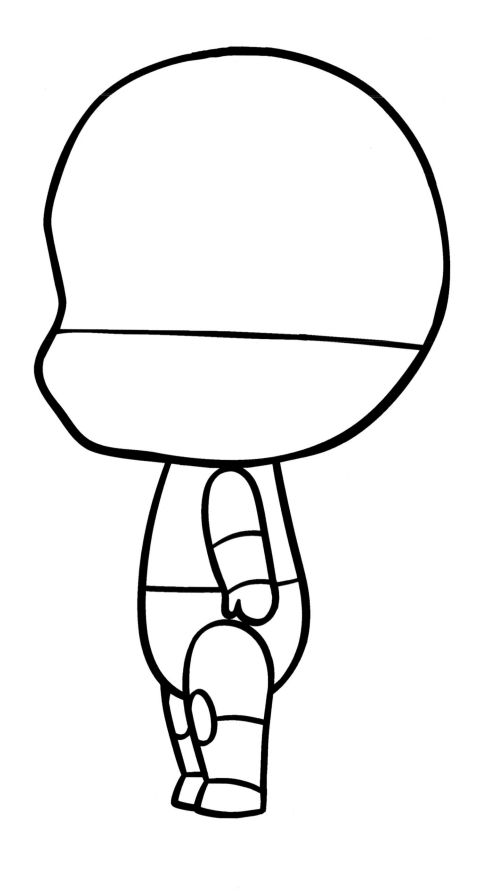

TWO-LEGGED CRITTER 3/4 VIEW

FOUR-LEGGED CRITTER FRONT VIEW

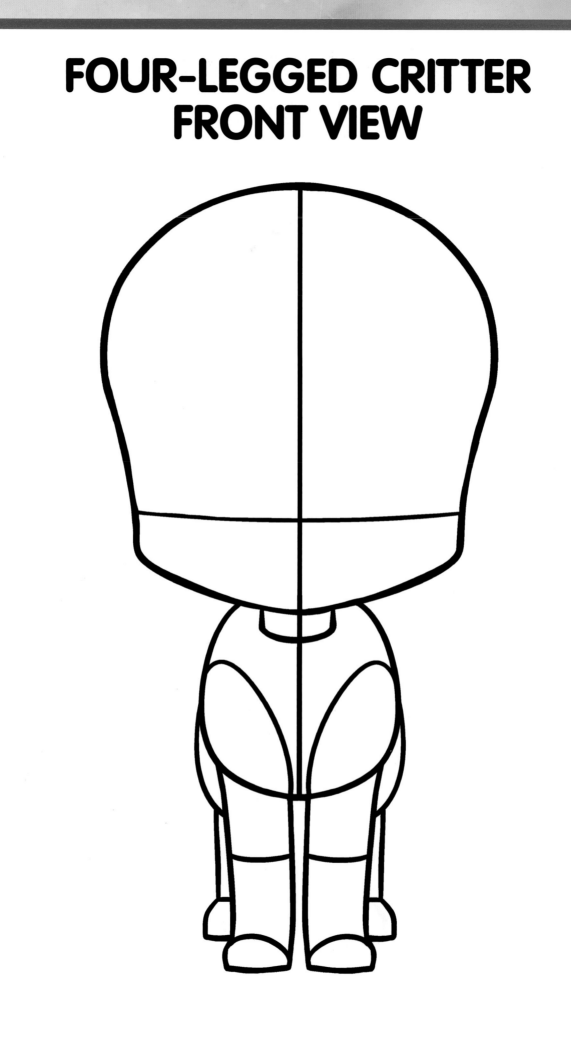

FOUR-LEGGED CRITTER
SIDE VIEW

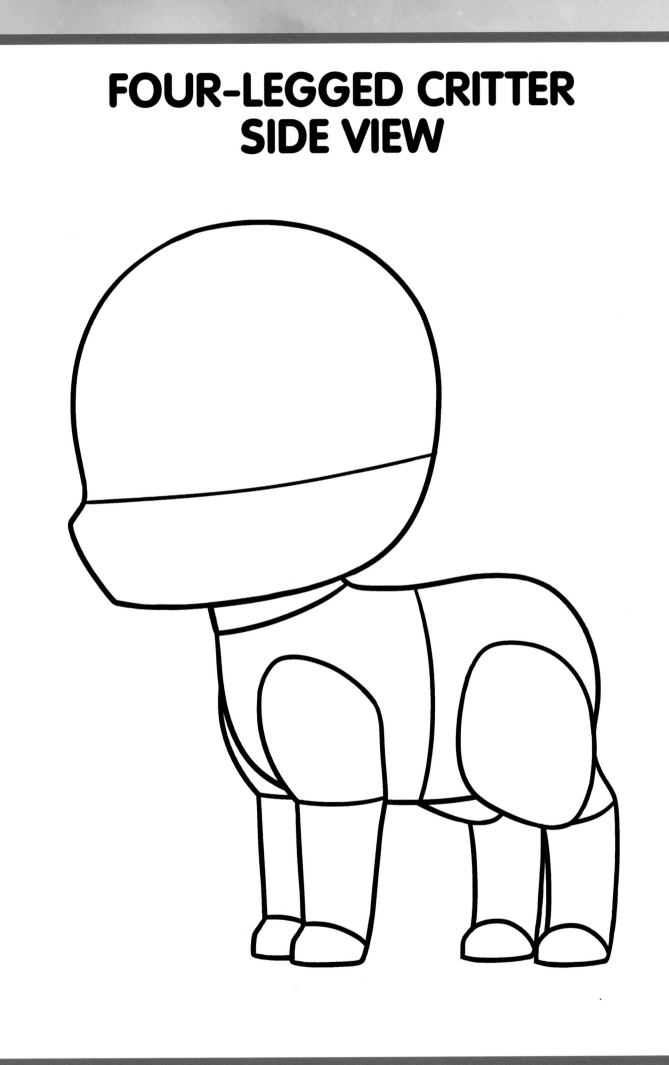

ABOUT THE ARTISTS

Samantha Whitten is a full-time freelance artist who specializes in creating art of adorable! She has spent all of her life drawing and has pursued a career in illustration and graphic design, learning on her own and dabbling in a variety of projects. These days she earns a living by selling a unique range of products featuring her artwork, employing a cute and fun style that appeals to all ages, as well as illustrating various web comics in her spare time. Visit www.littlecelesse.com.

Jeannie Lee considers herself an artist with many interests. She started drawing at a young age and eventually trained under contemporary fine artist Ji Young Oh for more than a decade. Jeannie studied traditional character animation at California Institute of the Arts, has held positions at Udon Entertainment and Marvel Comics, and has illustrated for Gaia Online (www.gaiaonline.com). She currently works as a lead artist at a small but growing company specializing in mobile games. Jeannie is the author of *How to Draw My Manga World*, also by Walter Foster.